Faith and Families

Faith and Families

Edited by
LINDELL SAWYERS

THE GENEVA PRESS

PHILADELPHIA

© 1986 The Geneva Press

Book design by Dorothy E. Jones

First edition

Published by The Geneva Press®

Philadelphia, Pennsylvania

PRINTED IN THE UNITED STATES OF AMERICA
2 4 6 8 9 7 5 3 1

Library of Congress Cataloging-in-Publication Data

Faith and families.

Papers from the Ghost Ranch Symposium on "Faith and
Families," held July 1–8, 1985.
Bibliography: p.
1. Family—Religious life—Congresses. 2. Church
work with families—Congresses. I. Sawyers, Lindell.
II. Ghost Ranch Symposium on "Faith and Families"
(1985).
BV4526.2.F313 1986   261.8′3585   86-3134
ISBN 0-664-24038-0 (pbk.)

Contents

Preface

The Ghost Ranch Symposium on "Faith and Families" began as a dream at the time of the reunion of two Presbyterian bodies in 1983 to form the Presbyterian Church (U.S.A.). A number of us on the New York and Atlanta staffs of the new church were especially concerned about the future of family ministry in our denomination and began to wonder how this important concern could be lifted up and enriched by the thinking of scholars and practitioners in the family field and other disciplines. Carol Rose Ikeler, my Atlanta counterpart in family ministry, and I also recognized that family ministry was the concern of many other church bodies. We share in the work of the National Council of Churches' Commission on Family Ministries and Human Sexuality, and our relationships there with persons of many denominations provided ample evidence that family ministry concerns are underfunded and understaffed in many sectors of the larger church. A symposium of the sort we were dreaming about would serve far wider interests than just those of Presbyterians.

The symposium became a reality. We met July 1–8, 1985, at "the Ranch," to share in the companionship of God's family in that place. Many of us came as families. We spoke, we listened, and we conversed about that which was so much a part of each person's existence: faith and family. A Focusing Statement, included at the end of this book, provided the broad framework for our discussions during the week.

In addition to the major presenters whose papers comprise this book, a participant-observer group of thirty heard the papers and shared in the dialogue. They were the voice of reality about the family and the messengers of hope for its future in church and society.

The papers tell their own story. They are the product not only of scholarship but of deep commitment on the part of the persons who presented them. In this book they are arranged in an order that moves from biblical and social research data to responses to these realities from the perspective of Christian existence. Among the many themes, I am particularly struck by two. The first theme is that of the importance of viewing family life, whatever its configuration or style, as a part of a larger community and of society. Families do not exist in isolation from the larger world (although, in our privatistic life-styles it may seem so); rather, they are part of an ecosystem that affects them deeply and that they affect. Health in families depends on how we learn to receive and give support within these larger environments, and, indeed, how we learn to change them so that they are health-giving.

A second major theme has to do with how families in all their variety can serve as contexts for growth in Christian faith. The family is an expression of our humanity, to be sure; it is part of the "created order." But the family is also a setting in which redemptive things can happen. God wills to be glorified in this aspect of creation. Our families, fragile as they seem, are nevertheless arenas in which persons can grow in faith and responsibility and, in so doing, praise their Maker.

There are many to be thanked for the success of the symposium and for the publication of this book. Only a few can be mentioned here. First, there is Carol Rose Ikeler, who supported the venture so fully and was prevented from attending the meetings because of surgery. A paper by her is included in the collection, even though she was unable to share personally in the proceedings. My heartfelt thanks, and Carol's also, to Lois Stover, regional communicator for the Synod of Florida, and formerly a staff person in Atlanta, for her willingness to serve in Carol's place as co-convener of the sessions. Her sensitivity to all present made the difference again and again as we planned and facilitated the sessions.

My thanks as well to Jim Hall, director of Ghost Ranch, for extending the hospitality of the Ranch to the presenters and their families, and to Robert D. McIntyre, director of the Publications Unit of the Program Agency, for supporting the publication venture. My thanks also to James G. Kirk, whose Office of Discipleship and Worship made it possible to have the voices of single persons and youth, and of black and Hispanic communities, present in our deliberations. I wish to thank Donald Brown and John C. Purdy of my own Church Education Services family for affirming the project and clearing many obstacles, and Robert H. Kempes, director of Unit III of the Program Agency, who has encouraged and supported my efforts in adult and family life education over many years.

Finally, thanks to Ruth, my life partner, who has interpreted to me the deepest meaning of family.

LINDELL SAWYERS
*Associate for Adult Education
and Family Ministries*

Faith and Families

1

Faith and Family
in Biblical Perspective

Judith Kovacs

Consider these familiar texts about the family.

God created man in his own image, in the image of God he created him; male and female he created them. And God blessed them, and God said to them, "Be fruitful and multiply."   —Gen. 1:27–28

Whoever divorces his wife and marries another, commits adultery against her; and if she divorces her husband and marries another, she commits adultery.   —Mark 10:11–12

As in all the churches of the saints, the women should keep silence in the churches. For they are not permitted to speak, but should be subordinate, as even the law says.   —1 Cor. 14:33–34

Now a bishop must be above reproach. . . . He must manage his own household well, keeping his children submissive and respectful in every way; for if a man does not know how to manage his own household, how can he care for God's church?   —1 Tim. 3:2–5

Honor your father and your mother, that your days may be long in the land which the LORD your God gives you.   —Ex. 20:12

Let the children come to me, do not hinder them; for to such belongs the kingdom of God.   —Mark 10:14

Most of us, if asked to speak about "biblical perspectives on the family," would be able to produce a few texts like those just quoted. Some of us might cite texts with which we agree, while others of us—for example, those who are active in the women's movement—might think first of the biblical texts that give us the most trouble. But what else can we say on this subject, beyond such proof-texting?

In this chapter I shall survey some of the wealth of biblical data relevant to the question of faith and family and indicate some of the exegetical and hermeneutical issues that the study of these texts raises. Some of the questions that I shall ask are the following:

1. How does the Bible present the relationship between faith and the family?
2. How do biblical authors use family imagery and family stories, and what are some of the implications of these images and stories?
3. What does the Bible have to say about the roles of men and women in the family? In a time when feminists have made us increasingly aware of the prevalence of patriarchy in the Bible, how are we to evaluate biblical statements on sex roles in marriage and in the church?

My aim is not to assemble a kind of biblical "how to" for the family, looking for specific moral guidance on such questions as how to discipline our children or what position the church should take on divorce. Instead, I will be asking how the family functions in biblical teaching, and how some of the broader concerns of the Bible might have a bearing on modern Christian families and on the church as a family of faith. My remarks will be divided into two main sections. In the first, I shall look at two different points of view on the relationship between faith and family, surveying a number of texts from both Testaments. In the second, I shall ask what the Bible has to say about the relationship of the sexes, with special focus on the letters of Paul.

Before we turn to the first of these two sections, a few general observations about the Bible are in order. When we approach the Bible with a specific question or theme in mind, one of the first things we are apt to notice is the great amount of diversity within sixty-six books. Of course there is unanimity on certain crucial assertions: for example, that God is one and that human beings should love God and their neighbors. But on many other important subjects the Bible does not speak with one voice. What we find in the Bible is not a distillation of timeless truths of the faith but rather a series of records of how the faithful—in Israel and in the early church—interpreted and reinterpreted their faith for the particular historical circumstances in which they found themselves. From historical-critical study of the Bible in the last century has emerged a fascinating picture of how Jews and Christians constantly updated and reapplied their sacred traditions—for example, the story of the exodus or the parables of Jesus—so that these might continue to be the *living* word of God.

We might say that the result of historical-critical study of the Bible is that we know both less and more than we thought we did. On the one hand, we are more aware of the complexity of the biblical material and the difficulty of stating the normative biblical position on many particular issues. On the other hand, we know a great deal more about the history of the biblical tradition, and about the specific communities and situations in which various parts of the tradition arose. This means that we may be frustrated if we go to the Bible expecting to find ready-made answers to our modern questions. It also means, however, that we are greatly enriched by having access not only to the biblical answers but also to the questions and situations to which the biblical authors spoke. This makes possible a deeper sense of community with the faithful in other ages.

One example of historical particularity of which we need to be aware is the understanding of the term "family." In our own time and culture we think of family primarily in terms of the so-called nuclear family. But this view of family is a fairly recent development; in other ages and cultures the term "family" designated many different forms of social reality.[1] For the ancient Israelites and early Christians, the primary sense of "family" was the extended family:

Since marriage was patriarchal—i.e., father-centered—among
the people of the Bible, the family was a community of persons,
related by ties of marriage and kinship, and ruled by the authority of the father. The biblical family, especially when marriage
was polygamous, was large. It included the father, mother(s),
sons, daughters, brothers, sisters (until their marriage), grandparents, other kinsmen, as well as servants, concubines, and so-
journers (aliens).[2]

The extended family of the Old Testament was characterized
not only by its size but also by its sharing of a common
residence. At least in the early days it was a self-sufficient
economic unit.[3] The "house of the father" had great importance in Old Testament times, providing the basis of the
larger social order of clans and tribes.

PART I: THE FAMILY AND FAITH—
TWO BIBLICAL VOICES

Let us turn now to the first question posed above: How does
the Bible present the relationship between faith and the
family? While there are many texts in the Bible that emphasize the positive relationship between faith and family, there
are others that picture that relationship as one of tension.
Passages that affirm the family are more familiar to most of
us. Both in the Old Testament and in the New, the community of faith is itself described as a family. In the early stories
of Abraham and Sarah, Isaac and Rebekah, Jacob and Ra-
chel, faith was quite literally a family affair. As the nation
of Israel grew, it was still understood as "the household of
God," and its worship was the worship of an extended family
or tribe (cf. Joshua 23 and 1 Samuel 1).

Since all the earliest Christians were Jews, it was quite
natural that they should take over the images of family and
household to describe their new religious community. As in
the days of Abraham, the wandering Aramean, the community was small and focused around a few family groups.
Paul's letters, the earliest books in the New Testament, contain greetings to and from Aquila and Prisca and the church

in their house (Rom. 16:5; 1 Cor. 16:19). He speaks of "the household of Stephanas" as "the first converts" in Greece (1 Cor. 16:15) and the very basis of the church there.

From Paul's letters and from the accounts of the early church in The Acts of the Apostles, we get a sense of the great importance of individual families for the fledgling church. They provided the locus of preaching, teaching, worshiping, and celebrating the Eucharist (Acts 2:2, 46; 5:42), and their help was crucial for the success of the early Christian mission, as the case of Paul himself shows. Before his conversion, when he persecuted the church, Paul went to "house after house" to search out Christians and drag them off to prison (Acts 8:3). In his later role as Christian missionary he likewise went from house to house, and he depended on the hospitality of such people as the missionary couple Priscilla and Aquila (Acts 18:3) and the woman called Lydia in Philippi, whom he baptized "with her household" (Acts 16:14–15). The story of Paul's imprisonment in Philippi (Acts 16) and several other stories in Acts indicate that such opening of one's house to the early Christian missionaries could be a risky business (cf. Acts 9:23–25; 18). Christians of later centuries owe much to the courage and faithfulness of these first Christian families.

It is not only these stories that have a bearing on our subject. The Bible uses many images from the realm of family life to refer to the faithful in their relationships with God and with each other. For example, Paul repeatedly refers to fellow Christians as "brothers" and "sisters," and on one occasion speaks of Christ as "the first-born among many brethren" (Rom. 8:29). He views his young churches as extended families, and at least once refers to himself as their father (1 Cor. 4:15).

More frequently, of course, the image of father is reserved for God. This brings us to the most common way the Bible uses family images—to describe the relationship between God and the believer. While the title "Father" is relatively infrequent in the Old Testament[4] in comparison with such titles as "Lord" and "King," it is very common in the New

Testament, especially in the Gospels. In fact, Jesus' characteristic reference to God as "Abba" ("Father" or "my Father") is one of the features of the Gospel narratives that has passed every test of historicity used in the different "quests" for the historical Jesus.[5]

The Bible also compares God to other family members. In Hosea, God appears as a faithful husband who goes after his errant wife Israel (Hosea 1 to 4). It is noteworthy that several Old Testament texts compare God to a mother. In a promise recorded in Isaiah 66, God is described as a nursing mother who dandles her children on her knees (vs. 12ff.). A similar use of the mother image to express God's faithful love to Israel is found in Isa. 49:15: "Can a woman forget her sucking child, that she should have no compassion on the son of her womb?" (cf. Num. 11:11–12; Deut. 32:11). The following passage from Hosea, which speaks of Yahweh's relationship to Israel as a parent-child relationship, also uses mother imagery:

> When Israel was a boy, I loved him; I called my son out of Egypt.
> . . . It was I who taught Ephraim to walk, I who had taken them in my arms, but they did not know that I harnessed them in leading-strings and led them with bonds of love, that I had lifted them like a little child to my cheek, that I had bent down to feed them. (Hos. 11:1–4)[6]

This text also illustrates the use of the image of "son" to describe Israel (cf. Ex. 4:22–23; Jer. 31:9); in other passages, the king is called God's adopted son (e.g., 2 Sam. 7:14; Ps. 2:7). In the New Testament the term "son" appears frequently, to refer not only to Jesus as the Son of God but also to the believer. In the Sermon on the Mount, Jesus promises: "Blessed are the peacemakers, for they shall be called *sons of God*" (Matt. 5:9, italics added). Paul says that Christians are called "sons of God" through adoption, when they have received the Holy Spirit:

> For all who are led by the Spirit of God are sons of God. For you did not receive the spirit of slavery to fall back into fear, but you

have received the spirit of sonship. When we cry, "Abba! Father!"
it is the Spirit [itself] bearing witness with our spirit that we are
children of God. (Rom. 8:14–16; cf. Gal. 4:4–7)

Before considering a few of the theological implications of
this family imagery, I want to call attention to one other
type of evidence of the importance of the family in the Bible,
namely, the extensive use of family stories to teach theology.
There is space to mention only a few of the many family
stories in the Bible—the vivid mythological and legendary
tales of Genesis and the amazingly candid accounts of
David's family life in 1 and 2 Samuel. The very first story in
the Bible, after the creation of the world, concerns the origin
of the family. In the ensuing chapters of Genesis we find the
story of the first murder, a fratricide, followed by other tales
of sibling rivalry (Jacob and Esau, Joseph and his brothers)
and trickery, redeemed at least partially by the surprising
forgiveness of the rogue Jacob by his offended brother Esau
(Gen. 33:4ff.).

The stories of David's family life provide a remarkable
counterbalance to the accounts of his public splendor and his
victories in battle. David's unprincipled passion for Bath-
sheba is known to all. Somewhat less familiar is the poignant
story of his relationship with his rebellious son Absalom.
Though forced to do battle against his son, David bitterly
laments his death: "O my son Absalom, my son, my son
Absalom! Would I had died instead of you, O Absalom, my
son, my son!" (2 Sam. 18:33). Such stories use the complexi-
ties of family life—the possibilities for alienation as well as
harmony—to teach about God and our relationship with
God, about sin and salvation.

Family tales are less common in the New Testament, but
there is at least one very influential example: Jesus' parable
of the prodigal son (Luke 15:11–32), which might be better
titled "the father's love." According to Luke, Jesus told this
story in answer to those who criticized him for associating
with the riffraff of society. Jesus teaches about God's forgive-

ness and love—which are mediated in his own ministry—by
telling a story about the extravagant actions of a loving
father toward his wayward son:

> But while [the son] was yet at a distance, his father saw him and
> had compassion, and ran and embraced him and kissed him.
> . . . [And] the father said to his servants, "Bring quickly the best
> robe, and put it on him; and put a ring on his hand, and shoes
> on his feet; and bring the fatted calf and kill it, and let us eat and
> make merry; for this my son was dead, and is alive again; he was
> lost, and is found." (Luke 15:20–24)

One obvious conclusion to be drawn from the Bible's predi-
lection for family stories and images is that faith has a lot
to do with family: God calls us in families, and our family
relationships are to be revelatory of God's love for us. Is this
observation too obvious even to be uttered? In biblical times
it was, but in our own secular and individualistic time perhaps it is not. Let me suggest some other implications of the
biblical data surveyed thus far. First, the texts, speaking to
us from quite different times and places in the church's history, call us to rethink our understanding of the church. As
children, many of us had the experience of being asked in
Sunday school to picture the church, only to be told when we
drew a building with a white steeple: "The church is not
really the building but the people." Perhaps we are more
capable now of understanding this point, but how easy it is
for us, who live in an age dominated by impersonal organizations, to continue thinking of the church primarily as an
institution or a building!

Of course we cannot and should not play what New Testament scholar Krister Stendahl has called the game of "First-
Century Bible land,"[7] and try to reverse nineteen centuries
of institutional developments in the church. The New Testament itself, in its later strata, suggests that at least some
institutionalization was necessary, as the house-churches became larger and the diversity of views became a serious
threat to the unity of the church (cf. 1 Timothy). But perhaps
we can try harder to maintain the tension between the two

New Testament views of the church: the house-church and the universal, institutional church. It may be time to revive the house-church, in the form of small communities of faith within larger congregations, groups centered in families or neighborhoods, where it is easier to practice "worship in everyday life" (cf. Romans 12).[8]

The house-church would be a place to be thoughtful and honest about the intersection between our theology and the particularities of our daily lives, just as it was when Paul wrote to the Corinthians and tried to explain to them what their sex lives and their handling of social invitations had to do with the central affirmations of the gospel. It would also be a place to ponder the particular way in which we, in our own time, are called, not to be "conformed to this world," but to "be transformed" (Rom. 12:2) and to be agents of transformation. Reports from the World Council of Churches project called Family Power Social Change give numerous examples of how such family-centered communities can serve as agents for constructive change, and James and Kathleen McGinnis have described their experience of the power of a small community of families gathering together for worship and social action.[9]

A second implication of the biblical data I have surveyed is that the biblical word for families is not contained solely, or even primarily, in the specific commandments about family life but rather in the central proclamations of the Bible. We can infer this from the way the bible uses family images and stories. The central question for Christian families is not "What are the biblical laws, or even the biblical models, for us?" but "How are we to live out our theology—the central affirmations of our faith—in the intimate spheres of our lives together?"

We are so accustomed to speaking of God as "Father" and ourselves as "children of God" that we rarely pause to think of what these words might mean. Why does the Bible use these terms, and why do biblical authors use so many family stories? Is it not to invite us to draw analogies, in both directions? The Bible suggests that we will understand something about God if we ponder the relationship between parents and children (cf. Luke 11:11–13). For example, as parents our concrete understanding of the relationship between love for our children and the need to discipline them may give us more real insight into our relationship with God than does some abstract statement about the interplay of God's justice and mercy. Likewise, we learn about how to live as parents and children by considering God's love for us.

The Bible suggests that the family is not only a subject for sociological analysis or a part of the social concern of the church but also a locus of revelation, a place for theological insight.[10] One rather disconcerting example of this for parents is the idea that, in some way they cannot entirely avoid, they stand as earthly analogies of God's love. Of course such analogies are not complete, as theologians over the centuries have pointed out and family therapists now are quick to agree. We need to beware of an overly anthropomorphic view of God. But our caution should not cause us to overlook the power of the analogy.

The use of the analogy of marriage to describe the relationship between Christ and the church is familiar to most people who attend weddings (cf. Ephesians 5). But an even more powerful use of marriage symbolism is found in The Book of Hosea, where the prophet, expressing his theology by analogy with his own family experience, describes Yahweh, the holy one of Israel, as a cuckolded husband, going after his errant wife in love (Hosea 1 to 4). Hosea's version of the good news of God's grace may be particularly relevant in our day, because it takes seriously the reality of broken relationships. Even these, suggests the prophet, can teach us something about God.

Let us turn now to another biblical view of faith and the family and look at some texts that speak of a tension between the two. This tension is evident already at the very beginning of the story of Israel, the account of the call of Abraham in Genesis 12. The part of this story we know best is the promise: Abraham will become a great nation and by him all the families of the earth will bless themselves. But

before the promise comes the challenge. God orders
Abraham: "Go from your country and your kindred and your
father's house to the land that I will show you." In a quite
literal journey of faith, Abraham is called to break his sacred
kinship ties and go out into the great unknown. Another
place where the cycle of stories about Abraham reflects this
tension between faith and family is the difficult story in
Genesis 22, in which God inexplicably commands Abraham,
"Take your son, your only son Isaac, whom you love" and
offer him up as a burnt sacrifice. The story turns out to have
a happy ending, and it provided early Christian allegorists
with an Old Testament foreshadowing of the cross. But it
still presents difficulties for both Jewish and Christian ex-
egetes by giving such a vivid example of how even the closest
of human ties is relativized by the presence of God.

Of the many other Old Testament stories that portray a
tension between faith and family, let me mention just two
others. The first comes from The Book of Ezra, an account of
the difficult new beginnings of the Jewish remnant after
their return from exile in Babylon. Ezra, a priest and scribe
zealous for the law of Yahweh and for the purity of God's
holy people, is appalled when he learns that some of those
who returned from exile have intermarried with non-Jews.
He makes them swear to put away not only their foreign
wives but also their children—which they hasten to do (Ezra
9 and 10). The narrator of The Book of Ezra, unlike the
earlier teller of the story of Abraham and Isaac, portrays
this momentous episode without any hint of emotion—save
for Ezra's vivid fear of the wrath of God. The fathers of Israel
voice no regret at casting off their own flesh and blood; they
betray no inner turmoil. But still we perceive the tension:
Israel may be viewed as a family, but it is a family as constituted by the command of God, not by human alliances, or
even by birth.

A final Old Testament example is set in a much earlier
time in Israel's history—in the time of judges, before there
was a king in Israel. It is a story best known by the great line:
"Entreat me not to leave you . . . ; for where you go I will go,

and where you lodge I will lodge; your people shall be my
people, and your God my God" (Ruth 1:16)—a line that
would be a perfect wedding text were it not spoken by one
woman to another woman. Ruth, the Moabite woman, addresses her mother-in-law, Naomi, after both have lost their
husbands in Moab and as Naomi is about to return to her
native land of Israel. It is a poignant example of family
loyalty, but behind the famous line is another break in kinship ties. Like Abraham, who leaves his father and his clan,
Ruth leaves her own mother, her people, and her native gods
to come "to a people that [she] did not know before" and take
refuge under the wings of the God of Israel (Ruth 2:11–12).
Although there is no report of a divine call to Ruth similar
to Abraham's, the end of the book makes it clear that God's
hand was involved in Ruth's momentous decision to desert
her parental family. For she was to become the great-grand-
mother of one of the most famous of Israel's sons—the great
king David.

The motif of tension between faith and family also appears
in the New Testament, especially in some of the sayings of
Jesus. The same Evangelist who records the parable of the
father's love for the prodigal son preserves the following
saying of Jesus:

> If any one comes to me and does not hate his own father and
> mother and wife and children and brothers and sisters, yes, and
> even his own life, he cannot be my disciple. (Luke 14:26)

This is a hard saying and one that most of us succeed in
ignoring altogether. That Christians have been able to make
anything of it at all is probably due to the fact that Matthew
has preserved a softer version of the saying:

> He who loves father or mother more than me is not worthy of me;
> and he who loves son or daughter more than me is not worthy of
> me. (Matt. 10:37)

While New Testament scholars will tell us that Luke's version is probably closer to Jesus' actual words,[11] there is some
doubt about which version better conveys Jesus' intent to a

later audience, who cannot hear the saying in its original setting. One solution is to say that Matthew has the main point right, while Luke has more correctly preserved Jesus' original tone.

If, however, we look to Matthew to do away with the offense of Jesus' teaching on family loyalties, we are in for a disappointment. For just before his softer version of the saying about hating one's family, Matthew records the following hard sayings:

> Do not think that I have come to bring peace on earth; I have not come to bring peace, but a sword. For I have come to set a man against his father, and a daughter against her mother, and a daughter-in-law against her mother-in-law; and a man's foes will be those of his own household. (Matt. 10:34–36; cf. Luke 12:51–53)

A related saying is found in Mark 13, in the context of Jesus' prophecy of the eschaton (the endtime):

> And brother will deliver up brother to death, and the father his child, and children will rise against parents and have them put to death; and you will be hated by all for my name's sake. (Mark 13:12–13; cf. Luke 21:16–17)

What are we to make of these texts and the many others in the Gospels that speak of tension between faith and family?[12] First, we need to be aware that here, as throughout the Gospels, we are dealing with more than one level of tradition. The early Christians did not regard the traditions about Jesus the way modern historians do but handed them on together with their own interpretations of the meaning of Jesus for their own time. Thus, for example, the sayings about divisions in households (Matt. 10:34–36) and about the handing over of parents, children, and siblings to trial and death (Mark 13:12) may tell us more about the result of Jesus' ministry than about its declared intention. A major theme of the New Testament is the division and strife between those who followed Jesus and those who regarded him as a dangerous impostor (see especially the Gospel of John). It is not surprising that such division should have

separated families as well, or that it would become particularly obvious and painful in times of persecution (cf. John 9;
1 Corinthians 7).

Some of the sayings about family strife, however, probably
do go back to the historical Jesus, and they serve to remind
us of an important aspect of Jesus' teaching—the fact that
he viewed his own mission as eschatological, that is, as God's
decisive challenge at the end of the age. In view of his expectation of an imminent consummation of world history, Jesus
issued a radical challenge to repent. A crucial issue for New
Testament hermeneutics is the question of how to interpret
Jesus' eschatological teaching in an age when most Christians do not share his expectation of the imminent end of the
world. Can we remain true to the radicality of Jesus' message without sharing his eschatological views? One value of
the hard saying in Luke 14:26 about the need to hate one's
parents in order to be Jesus' disciple is that it reminds us of
the radical nature of Jesus' teaching. Matthew's softened
version of the saying, which exhorts us to love Jesus more
than our parents, may be a useful interpretation of Jesus'
saying for the purpose of general moral exhortation. Several
stories in the Gospels make clear that Jesus was not an
enemy of family life; for example, consider the famous inci-
dent in which he sanctions marriage and changes the Old
Testament law allowing divorce (Mark 10:2–10), and his
blessing of the children (Mark 10:13–14). The limitation of
Matthew's version, however, is that it lacks the element of
radical challenge. Luke's more offensive version reminds us
of how easy it is to domesticate the gospel and underestimate
the tension between the Word of God and the ordinary values of the world.

Perhaps the meaning of Jesus' command is something like
what Paul has to say about the law (cf. Romans 7). Paul
realized that the most dangerous temptation to sin lies not
in the things that are clearly recognized as evil but in things
that are truly good. The Pharisees took offense at Jesus
because in breaking the law he attacked what they regarded
as supremely good. We tend to forget that the Pharisees are

not the only ones to be subject to this sort of sin, or to take offense at Jesus' radical call. Jesus' words about family enmity are not to be taken as law but as pointed warnings. If we pride ourselves on our harmonious family life, are we letting our family become a sort of protective cover that keeps us from taking seriously our commitment to God and our call to minister to the rest of the world? There is a danger of putting the value of "the good Christian family" in place of the central message of the gospel. At the same time, this danger exists only because family is clearly a good thing, as the Bible elsewhere recognizes.

What conclusions can we draw from this survey of biblical texts on faith and the family? The most obvious conclusions are, first, that family is an important theme in the Bible, and second, that there is a great deal of diversity in the evaluation of family and the treatment of the relationship between faith and family. Families were important in the origins of biblical faith—both in the Old Testament and in the New Testament. Family images and stories are frequently used to express theology. By drawing analogies between family relationships and relationships with God, biblical authors underline the importance of family life, not only as a concern for practical ethics but also as a place of revelation—a place where we can come to understand our proper relation to God. But the Bible also speaks of tension between faith and family. While the family partakes of the goodness of creation (Genesis 1), no created thing is to take precedence over God, and God is free to call persons out of their natural family relationships. The challenge of Jesus' preaching of "the kingdom of God" is radical, calling into question not only the religion of the holy law but also all human loyalties. Jesus expects us to give good gifts to our children, to support our parents, to remain loyal to our husbands and wives, but above all to follow him and to seek God's reign on earth.

In this survey I have deliberately avoided going to the Bible to look for specific rules on concrete moral issues. What position should the church take on divorce? on abortion? on homosexuality? These are important issues for us, and we need to consider them in the light of the whole biblical witness. But in doing so, we need to avoid proof-texting (taking one voice as normative for the whole biblical tradition) and anachronism (trying to apply to all times a teaching given for a specific situation).

In the next section, I shall focus on the third question I raised at the beginning of this paper, the question of how we are to interpret biblical statements on sex roles in the family and in the church. Taking the letters of Paul as a test case, I shall look briefly at how texts from Paul have been used in recent debates about sex roles. Then I shall try to broaden the basis of this debate by looking at Paul's general approach to ethical questions. It is my contention that twentieth-century Christians can learn a great deal from Paul, provided we do not try to make his specific advice into law but instead reflect on the basic affirmations of his theology and ethics.

PART II: FAITH, PATRIARCHY, AND FEMINISM

In recent years our churches have seen much discussion of biblical texts relevant to the roles of the sexes in family and church. Some Christians have argued that the Bible gives one clear, normative pattern for Christian family life—a patriarchal pattern in which authority is exercised by father and husband over wife and children—and that this pattern is as valid for our own times as it was in the first century. Support for this view is found especially in passages from the later epistles of the New Testament—for example, the "household codes" in Eph. 5:21 to 6:9; Col. 3:18 to 4:1; and 1 Peter 2:11 to 3:12, and the rules for the church in the three pastoral epistles (1 and 2 Timothy and Titus). In addition, there are two frequently cited passages from Paul's first letter to the Corinthians (1 Cor. 11:1–16 and 14:33–36) that reflect a patriarchal view of relationships between the sexes, and limit women's activity in worship. Christians who emphasize these texts feel that the church should be actively concerned to reinforce the specifically Christian pattern of family life which they outline. They argue that we have here the clear command of the Bible, and further, that the biblical pattern provides an antidote to the contemporary breakdown of the family.

Other Christians, who are concerned to promote the equality of women and men, view these texts, and the many other biblical texts that reflect a patriarchal view of the family, as an offense and a serious hermeneutical problem. Some even argue that the oppression of patriarchy so dominates the Bible as to call into question its authority and relevance for twentieth-century Christians.[13]

Neither of these approaches is adequate. One problem with the first point of view is that it is based on a simplistic understanding of the inspiration of the Bible, ignores the diversity in the Bible, and rules out the kind of reexamining and updating of traditions that are attested in the Bible itself. The second position, for its part, is based on an exaggerated respect for modernity and a corresponding contempt for the biblical point of view. It implies that because we have learned much from the social sciences, we have nothing to learn from the Bible.

It is possible to take another approach to the biblical teachings about family life, one that takes the Bible seriously but also takes seriously the new insights and challenges of our own time. Biblical scholars, in dialogue with feminism, have suggested some new directions, for example, by calling attention to the importance of women within the biblical tradition and to parts of the Bible that go against the prevailing patriarchal trend. In her recent book, *In Memory of Her,* Elisabeth Schüssler Fiorenza attempts to show that Jesus challenged the patriarchal family and that independent women had a considerably greater role in Christian origins than has been recognized. She argues that the passages in the later New Testament epistles that commend patriarchy do not express a distinctively Christian view of the family but instead reflect adaptation of the gospel to the prevailing patriarchal views of first-century Greco-Roman culture, an adaptation that was made in response to particular historical circumstances.[14]

If we are interested in a serious exploration of what the Bible has to say about the structure of the family in our own time, we need to take account of feminist biblical scholarship, which has posed clearly the issue of patriarchy in the Bible and increased our awareness of the diversity of biblical views and of the interaction between biblical teaching and the cultures of the times in which the Bible was written. In addition, we need to explore our concrete questions about family roles in the light of a broader understanding of the central teaching of the Bible. I shall attempt to give a preliminary sketch of such an interpretation in the case of Paul.

In his own day, Paul was a figure of controversy, and he continues to be in ours, awakening strong opposition and even hatred in some and devotion in others. Exegesis of Paul has figured heavily in recent debates on the role of women in the family and in the church. While many, subscribing to George Bernard Shaw's view of Paul as "the archenemy of women," hold Paul responsible for the oppression of women in the church, others use texts from Paul to argue for the equality of women with men in the family and in the church, even going so far as to assert that Paul is "the only certain and consistent spokesman for the liberation and equality of women in the New Testament."[15]

How are such differing assessments possible? There are two main reasons. First, some of the texts that have most influenced the church's perspective on women are found in the pastoral letters, which for centuries had been regarded as the work of Paul but are now generally regarded by biblical scholars to be the product of a follower of Paul writing several decades after Paul.[16] The following passage from 1 Timothy, for example, has been a key text for the view of Paul as "the archenemy of women":

I desire then that in every place the men should pray . . . ; also that women should adorn themselves modestly and sensibly in seemly apparel . . . by good deeds, as befits women who profess religion. . . . Let a woman learn in silence with all submissiveness. I permit no woman to teach or to have authority over men; she is to keep silent. For Adam was formed first, then Eve; and Adam was not deceived, but the woman was deceived and became a transgressor. Yet woman will be saved through bearing children, if she continues in faith and love and holiness, with modesty. (1 Tim. 2:8–15)

This text, with its demand for the subordination of women in the family and their exclusion from leadership in the church, and its emphasis on female responsibility for human sin, has had considerable effect on the status of women in home and church. But it was not written by Paul, and we need consciously to disregard this text and its later influence if we want to get clear about Paul's view of the role of women.

Yet even if we limit ourselves to the seven letters regarded by a great number of biblical scholars as having been written by Paul in the mid–first century (1 Thessalonians, Galatians, 1 and 2 Corinthians, Philippians, Philemon, and Romans), there is still room for different assessments of Paul's view of women. The second reason for the current debate about Paul's view of women is simply that the evidence in Paul's own letters is mixed. As noted above, there are two well-known passages in 1 Corinthians in which Paul presupposes a hierarchical view of the relationship between husband and wife and limits the role of women in worship:

But I want you to understand that the head of every man is Christ, the head of a woman is her husband, and the head of Christ is God. . . . Any woman who prays or prophesies with her head unveiled dishonors her head. . . . [But] a man ought not to cover his head, since he is the image and glory of God; but woman is the glory of man. For man was not made from woman, but woman from man. Neither was man created for woman, but woman for man. . . . Nevertheless, in the Lord woman is not independent of man nor man of woman; for as woman was made from man, so man is now born of woman. And all things are from God. (1 Cor. 11:3–12)

As in all the churches of the saints, the women should keep silence in the churches. For they are not permitted to speak, but should be subordinate, as even the law says. If there is anything they desire to know, let them ask their husbands at home. For it is shameful for a woman to speak in church. (1 Cor. 14:33–35)

On first glance, these texts seem to give a clear picture of Paul as an advocate of patriarchy in the home and in the church. But a closer look at these and other Pauline texts indicates that the picture is more complex. Many scholars believe that the passage in 1 Corinthians 14 is a later inter-polation into Paul's letter.[17] Even if it is original, it is hard to reconcile the advice it gives to what Paul says in 1 Corinthians 11, where he does not restrict women's right to speak in the assembly but only tells them to dress in a certain way when they prophesy. In addition, the text about female prophets (1 Cor. 11:1–16) is notoriously difficult to interpret; a good deal of scholarly attention has not yet resolved questions about the exact problem addressed, the logic of Paul's argument, and the meaning of specific words and phrases.

To complicate further the question of Paul's views on women and family structure, there are other texts that suggest a view of the relationship of the sexes which is quite different from the patriarchal attitude of 1 Corinthians 11 and 14. Those who view Paul as a spokesman for the equality of women appeal particularly to the following verses from Paul's letter to the Christians in Galatia:

> For as many of you as were baptized into Christ have put on Christ. There is neither Jew nor Greek, there is neither slave nor free, there is neither male nor female; for you are all one in Christ Jesus. (Gal. 3:27–28)

Further, in his discussion of marital sex in 1 Corinthians 7, Paul takes great care—even to the point of stylistic awk-wardness—to address both husband and wife equally, and he gives them the same advice: "For the wife does not rule over her own body, but the husband does; likewise the husband does not rule over his own body, but the wife does" (1 Cor. 7:4). The tone of this passage is markedly different from that of the later "household codes."

Schüssler Fiorenza has called attention to some other important but easily overlooked evidence about Paul's attitude toward women which is found in the greetings at the end of his letters. In Romans 16, for example—a text most of us never read because it is made up largely of proper names— Paul's list of esteemed co-workers begins with the deacon and protector (or "helper") Phoebe and includes names of at least five other women who have labored together with Paul for the sake of the gospel. In Phil. 4:2ff. he names two females who "have labored side by side" with him "in the gospel," together with two males, as leaders of a house-church. As in 1 Corinthians 7, the absence of a hierarchical treatment of male and female is striking; Paul makes no distinction between the kind of work done by female and male co-workers.

Thus while two passages in the Pauline corpus suggest patriarchy, several other texts suggest that in theory and especially in practice, Paul was closer to the idea of the equality of the sexes than to the patriarchal views prevalent in his own day. What can we learn from Paul as we think about the structure of the Christian family in the twentieth century? First, the very fact that various Pauline texts on the subject of women are hard to reconcile with each other is significant. For these texts provide a concrete example of the problems involved when we look to the Bible for eternally valid rules or clear-cut answers to our modern problems. While we don't know all the specifics of the situation addressed in Paul's first letter to the Corinthians, it is clear that Paul's advice about the role of women was tailored to this concrete situation. The fact that Paul's ethics are situational does not mean, however, that no general principles are involved, which would mean that persons in different circumstances from his immediate audience have nothing to learn from him. While his concrete advice may not apply to us in twentieth-century America, his general approach to the problem of living out our faith in our everyday lives clearly does.

It is ironic that passages from Paul's letters have made their way into church law, since Paul himself insists that the gospel is not a new law but proclamation of good news. For

Paul, ethics are based on theology, that is, on an understanding of what God has done, is doing, and will do for God's
people. When Paul is asked about a matter of Christian
praxis, his characteristic response is not to appeal to commands of Jesus but instead to recall the central affirmations
of his theology—the gospel of Jesus' death and resurrection
(cf. 1 Cor. 1:17ff.; 7:23; Gal. 3:1).

Twentieth-century Christians, no less than those in the
first century, need to be reminded of the radical nature of a
theology revealed in the death and resurrection of God's Son.
Paul portrays the cross of Christ as a judgment on all the
powers and standards of this world (cf. Gal. 6:14–15; 3:13; 1
Cor. 1:17ff.), not only the "principalities and powers" which
everyone recognizes as evil but also things such as the holy
law of the Jews and the exalted wisdom of Greek philosophy.[18] In our own time, the cross calls into question not only
legalism and patriarchy but also the other ideologies by
which we live—materialism, secularism, and individualism.
Even feminism is not exempt. The gospel calls us to ask what
God might be doing in our history in the light of what God
has done in the past—to consider, for example, to what extent the increased emancipation of women in our own century is in accord with, and serving of, the gospel. We need to
ask how all of these ideologies can alienate us from God and
from each other and thus come into conflict with the cross
of Christ.

Feminists have documented how the adaptation of the
gospel to serve patriarchy has led to centuries of oppression
of women in the church.[19] I like to think that Paul, were he
to write to us today, would welcome the increased freedom
of women in church and family and agree with New Testament scholar Robert Hamerton-Kelly, who asserts that the
shift in family structure in our time from "patriarchy to
partnership" is "the action of God in our history."[20] But Paul
would also caution that even in this positive development—
precisely because feminism is a good thing—there lies considerable danger of perverting the gospel. Like Jewish law
or Greek philosophy, feminism can become another system

by which human beings attempt to secure their own salvation (or "wholeness") and through which they exclude themselves from fellowship with persons who are not ritually or ideologically pure.

Thus far I have called attention to three insights of Paul that I think are relevant to twentieth-century moral and social questions, in particular to the question of sexual roles: first, Paul's situational approach to ethics; second, his insistence that the gospel not be made into a new legal system; and third, his understanding of the potential for enslavement and alienation in all human powers and ideologies and his understanding of the cross as judgment on them all. I have argued that the specific advice that Paul gives about sexual roles in 1 Corinthians is not particularly relevant to our own reflections about the Christian family some nineteen centuries later, but that Paul's proclamation of the gospel is still timely—and extremely important.

Several other key themes in Paul's letters that are relevant to our present questions are freedom, love, unity, and edification, or "building up" (cf. especially 1 Corinthians 5 to 14).

> For freedom Christ has set us free; stand fast therefore, and do not submit again to a yoke of slavery." (Gal. 5:1)

> For though I am free from all . . . , I have made myself a slave to all, that I might win the more. (1 Cor. 9:19)

In 1 Corinthians and in Galatians, in response to two very different situations, Paul speaks of Christian freedom, pleading with the Galatians not to give up their freedom in Christ to become slaves to the Jewish law and telling the freewheeling, enthusiastic Corinthians that they may have to limit their own freedom for the good of the church. We are fortunate that both of these letters have been preserved, for they show quite different sides of Paul's teaching, both of which have something to say to us. I have already discussed how Paul's arguments against Christian legalism are relevant to our own considerations of roles in the family. His response to the Corinthian individualists may be even more timely. In a recent issue of *Concern,* Robert Bellah has written about how the "rampant individualism" of our time has contributed to the breakdown of the family:

> This secular freedom, which is the heart of American individualism, and which is so powerful today, undermines, at least potentially, every human commitment and every human memory—walk away and don't look back. . . . Thus marriage, friends, job, community, church are all dispensable—I can always find others who will meet my needs, or if I don't it's my tough luck.[21]

Although many of us have an unprecedented degree of freedom, it has not necessarily led to personal happiness or to a better society. Our freedom often turns out to be freedom from rather than freedom for. Paul insists on the freedom of the Christian, but he also asserts, paradoxically, that people are always slaves—the only question is to what power one is enslaved:

> When you were slaves of sin, you were free in regard to righteousness. . . . But now . . . you have been set free from sin and have become slaves of God. (Rom. 6:20–22)

"Slaves of God"—this phrase may not be too popular in a time when Christians are rightly involved in struggles for liberation of the oppressed. But for this very reason it may be particularly valuable for us as a reminder of the scandal of the gospel, and its foreignness to the values of the world. It reminds us that even the highest human values, such as freedom, stand under judgment. The testimony of the Bible —from Genesis to Revelation—is that the human being is not a totally free, autonomous being. As we struggle to eliminate human relationships of dominance, such as patriarchy, we must not confuse the human dream of utopia and the kingdom of God. The book of Exodus has its place in between Genesis and Romans; the story of divine liberation is set in the context of an understanding of the pervasiveness of human sin. As we work for liberation from human oppression, we do so as slaves of the God who desires justice.

> For you were called to freedom, [brothers and sisters]; only do not
> use your freedom as an opportunity for the flesh, but through
> love be [slaves] of one another. (Gal. 5:13)

If Paul reminds us of our dependence on God, he also calls
us to concern for the family of faith; we are to be slaves not
only to God but to each other. Such language is open to
misuse, as is demonstrated by centuries of use of the Bible
to justify the institutions of slavery and patriarchy. But misuse implies that there is a proper use as well. In the church
we are all called to be "slaves" of each other; we are not to
let our concern for individual rights destroy the fellowship
of the body of Christ.

In 1 Corinthians, Paul focuses again and again on the
question of community. One of the best-known texts from
Paul is the hymn on love in 1 Corinthians 13. This text is
directed to a Christian community that was divided because
of differences in social status and because of the claims of
some to have special knowledge and superior charismatic
powers. Paul's hymn is not a sentimental outpouring but a
challenge to all forms of human arrogance and selfishness. "If
I have all faith, so as to remove mountains, but have not love,
I am nothing" (v. 2). Does not this have something to say to
those Christians who would boast of their own strong faith,
and see themselves as the inheritors of the only true Christian view of the family? "Love bears all things, believes all
things, hopes all things, endures all things" (v. 7). Some of us
may have trouble hearing this word, because of the tendency
of the church to apply admonitions to endurance and pa-
tience only to certain groups of people—for example, more to
women than to men. But Paul addresses this word to all—rich
and poor, sophisticated and simple, male and female.

Just before his hymn on love Paul uses the metaphor of
the body to emphasize the unity and interdependence of all
members of the church:

> For just as the body is one and has many members, and all the
> members of the body, though many, are one body, so it is with
> Christ. (1 Cor. 12:12)

Paul makes several points by means of this image. If one suffers, all suffer. The members of the community who seem to be "weaker and less honorable" are no less important for the life of the body. All members of the church should exercise the same care and concern for each other.

A final theme in 1 Corinthians to which I would like to call attention is Paul's repeated reminder to be concerned for the "edification" or "building up" of the church:

> "Knowledge" puffs up, but love builds up. (1 Cor. 8:1)

> "All things are lawful," but not all things are helpful. (1 Cor. 10:23)

> Then let us no more pass judgment on one another, but rather decide never to put a stumbling block or hindrance in the way of a brother. . . . Let us then pursue what makes for peace and for mutual upbuilding. (Rom. 14:13, 19)

Paul applies the metaphor of building up to different situations in his churches—to the schisms created by people who claimed superior wisdom, to the arrogance of those who boasted of speaking in tongues, and to divisions over questions of table fellowship and ritual purity. On these questions, Paul does not lay down the law but instead allows his churches freedom—a freedom in which the exercise of individual rights is tempered by a concern to encourage the faith of one's Christian brothers and sisters.

We might also apply this image to the divisions in the contemporary church over questions of family structure and sex roles. Women who feel oppressed by the church may find it particularly hard to consider this advice. As we struggle to win equal standing in the family and in the family of faith, it is difficult to think first of the community—especially when the community includes people whom we regard as oppressors.[22] But Paul challenges us to think not only of our own new insights or our own particular cause but also of how to foster unity and how to build up, not destroy, the church. Paul's discussions of edification also challenge people who insist that the church cling to the patriarchal model of the family and to established patterns of church leadership which restrict the role of women. Those who would defend the patriarchal view of family as central to the faith need to ask whether they are not putting up a stumbling block for other members of the body of Christ—and whether they are not missing some of the most basic teachings of the Bible, even as they try valiantly to be faithful to specific commandments.

I have suggested that the basic principles of Paul's ethics —his idea that ethics flow from theology, and his emphasis on freedom, love, unity, and mutual building up—are still important for the church today as well as for the individual Christian family. Paul's approach to ethical questions is quite different from that of most later Christians, in that it is not legalistic, nor is it based on any institutionalized authority. It will work only if Paul's guidelines are taken seriously by all members of the Christian family—by those who would conserve established patterns as well as by those who are trying to reform them. There is need for charity and humility in all quarters. In Christ there is no Jew or Greek, slave or free, male or female—patriarch or feminist—but we are all one.

2

Families in Church and Society: Sociological Perspectives

Janet Huber Lowry

In any study of human behavior it is helpful to set the stage by a careful description of facts about the past and a clear delineation of important trends. This chapter reviews the demographic information about families in the United States that can assist in drawing appropriate conclusions about changes and their impact. The discussion also considers recent studies about one church body, the Presbyterians, in order to allow a comparison with national trends and to distinguish unique features of these families. Finally, it interprets the important findings as they relate to faith and ministry within the church and our society.

THE BIG PICTURE—AMERICAN MARRIAGE AND FAMILY DEMOGRAPHY

While most sociologists recognize the post–World War II baby boom (generally those born from 1945 to 1959) as an aberration in the century-long decline in fertility levels in the United States, much of the public lives with the family

I wish to thank Dan Schores, Harry Smith, and Ted Wardlaw for comments and suggestions on earlier drafts. I also owe considerable debt to Presbyterian church families in Indiana, New York, North Carolina, and Texas as well as to my own family in California, Georgia, Illinois, Indiana, Michigan, Pennsylvania, New Hampshire, and Texas.

images of that era as normal. This disjuncture accounts for some of the alarm expressed in the 1960s and 1970s over the death of the family. Clearly the contemporary family is quite different in size, composition, and particularly in function from the family of more traditional rural America. The family is increasingly responsible beyond basic maintenance for personal emotional development, yet it is increasingly varied in the form, size, and command of resources with which to accomplish this purpose. The changes since World War II didn't create new or unprecedented forms until the early 1970s. Lower fertility had happened earlier, higher age at marriage wasn't that unusual in our past, nor was the proportion of persons who never married out of line with figures of about 10 percent common earlier in this century.

The increasing number, distribution, and diversity of households in America was the major demographic fact of the 1970s. These changes occurred from a confluence of many separate demographic trends. First, the marriage squeeze and the subsequent delayed marriage trend, particularly because it occurred to the largest age group ever in the United States, required more households for single or unrelated young adults living independently of their parents. (Marriage squeeze refers to the imbalance of young adults in the pool for first marriage, women and slightly older men, when a larger group follows a smaller group—1953–1955 versus 1950–1952.) Second, the declining (or more controlled) fertility reduced household size and aged our society more quickly. Third, the increased longevity of older persons, combined with the mobility of younger generations, meant that more elderly were continuing to maintain homes, especially older women. Fourth, greater incidence of divorce multiplied household demand, and increasing acceptance of single-parenting postponed the previous rush to marriage of many in these circumstances. Fifth, the great urban concentration began to turn around as nonmetropolitan areas saw the higher growth rates for the first decade since the great westward expansion of the previous century. Finally, this urban shift, combined with differing regional growth patterns, changed the scene of many households. These factors combined to produce the first decade in which the population growth rate declined while the household growth rate increased. The result was more households, more persons living alone, more different families, more nonurban settings, and more regional change variations.

The diversity of households is especially noteworthy. In gauging it, one must balance the amount and the rate of change (see table). Though they still constitute a small proportion of all households, unmarried couples or cohabiting

Households and Population by Household Type, U.S. 1970 and 1983— Number, Percentage Distribution and Change

(Note that the percentage of change is based on the difference in number between 1970 and 1983, not on the difference in percentage.)

| | Households | | | Population in | | |
	1970	1983	% Change	1970	1983	% Change
Number (in thousands)	63,401	83,918	32	199,384	229,178	15
Household type						
with children	45%	37%	−7%	66%	54%	−7%
without children under 18	55	63	53	34	46	56
Married couple	70	59	12	82	73	2
with own children	40	29	−5	60	46	−11
with none	30	30	33	22	27	36
One parent	5	8	102	6	8	43
mother only	4	7	100	5	7	42
father only	1	1	116	1	1	48
Living alone	17	23	80	6	8	80
women	11	14	63	4	5	63
men	6	9	116	2	3	116
Unmarried couple	1	2	262	1	2	266
Other	7	8	56	5	9	89
Total	100%	100%		100%	100%	

SOURCE: Adapted from Tables 1 and 2 in Paul C. Glick, "American Household Structure in Transition," *Family Planning Perspectives,* Vol. 16, No. 5 (September/October 1984), pp. 206–207. Based on U.S. Census *Current Population Reports.*

couples more than tripled since 1970. Part of the tremendous increase is related to the baby boom cohort's participation. (Cohort describes people with a common demographic fact; in this case, those born from 1945 to 1959 are the baby boom cohort.) For many, cohabiting is a new stage of intimacy preceding marriage at a later age. Fewer such households contain children than in 1960, 28 percent now versus 45 percent then, and more have adults under age forty-five than in 1960, 83 percent now versus 30 percent then.[1] There is an interesting complexity to these new kinds of couples. Among these urban young adults, according to Andrew Cherlin, there is "a better-educated group who tend to cohabit prior to marrying, and a less-well-educated group whose relationships are more likely to include at least one previously married partner."[2]

One-parent households, though also a small percentage of all households, showed a substantial increase, doubling since 1970. Of these single parents, only one in ten is a father, but the latter households are generally more affluent. They can afford the child care required and are more attractive remarriage candidates.[3] Single-parenting is increasingly within the sphere of divorce rather than separation, since the period of the latter has shortened considerably in recent years. However, from another angle single-parenting is a choice independent of marriage for a growing number of never marrieds. Population figures echo these changes, though change is less substantial for persons in one-parent households. It is interesting that "father only" households are increasing as rapidly as "mother only" households. Also important in this table is the declining prevalence of parents living with children—now only 37 percent of the households or 54 percent of the population lives with children under eighteen present. Marriage characterizes only three out of five households, or the living situation for only 75 percent of the population. The portion of persons who live alone also displayed considerable growth in the 1970s. Most households in the "Other" category of census tables are headed by women and represent such unusual family groups as a grandparent with a grandchild or grandchildren, sibling groups, or unrelated adults (two of the same sex or three or more of any sex combination).

Adding to the complexity of America's families is the reconstituted or blended or step-family produced by remarriage. Though these situations in today's world result from divorce rather than death, the incidence of marital dissolution until the 1970s has been comparable with earlier times when death and desertion were the most common causes. The greater pool of divorced persons today means that remarriage is on the rise. Whereas a third of all new marriages in 1970 were remarriages for one or both of the partners, almost 45 percent of all new marriages involve this today. In 1980 this meant that "20% of all existing marriages included at least one previously divorced spouse."[4] Such stepfamilies involved ten million children in 1978, or approximately "one out of every eight children living in a two-parent family."[5]

While none of us live in neighborhoods with such extreme heterogeneity, it might help to try to picture the hypothetical neighborhood of 10 households (H) and 27 persons (P) in America today (see diagram). Two from each category come from persons living alone, probably an elderly widow and a young divorced man (2 H, 2 P). Another household is the elderly couple on the corner (1 H, 2 P, and thus accounting for the 11 percent elderly). Five other homes have married couples, but only three represent young families with five dependent-age children split between them fairly evenly. One of these young families involves a remarriage and some nonresidential children. One of these probably has young adult children who attend the local community college or work part-time in the community (3 H, 12 P). Of the other two older married couples, one is at the empty nest stage, but the other has a twenty-eight-year-old still living at home (2 H, 5 P). The latter might also have Hispanic ethnicity for two of its members, accounting for the 6 percent of that growing minority. In the remaining two households we might find a young black mother with two dependent children and per-

A "TYPICAL" AMERICAN NEIGHBORHOOD

10 Households with 27 Persons

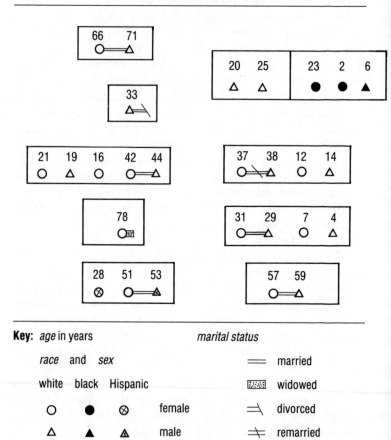

Key: *age* in years   *marital status*

race and *sex*   === married

white   black   Hispanic   ▩ widowed

O   ●   ⊗   female   �230 divorced

△   ▲   ⚠   male   ≠ remarried

Factors are depicted with as much accuracy as possible. Age (within five years) and sex are true for the population and the youth dependency for households. Race is accurate for both the population and the households. Marital status is accurate by broad categories—married/not married/remarried—for households and close for the population even in lesser categories. None of the other combinations (race and age) can be true with so few units. Household size is accurate. Three of the persons would be gay. Each rectangle, separate or adjoining, represents a household.

haps two young people sharing an apartment (2 H, 6 P, and thus accounting for the 11 percent black, also rounding out to about 26 percent under age eighteen in the neighborhood and the fourth household with children present). Try to picture yourself in this neighborhood. Residential patterns would seldom supply such diversity, but the clearly different needs of people and stages of life and types of households demonstrate the complexity with which Americans live in today's world. In such a microcosm of society each major division (age, sex, race, marital status, size of household) can be accurately represented even though the combinations (all blacks are under age twenty-five or all Hispanics are over twenty-five or all singles are either divorced or widowed) cannot depict the real variety.

These facts about families suggest that communities are growing more diverse. However, the momentum of change is slowing as the baby boom cohort ages. Paul Glick notes that "the demographic base for first marriages has already started to decline, and the demographic base for divorce will start to decline within a decade."[6] We can expect marriage rates, both first marriage and remarriage, to stabilize. Divorce rates, which have risen a lot, will fluctuate around the current levels of 20 to 24 per 1,000 marriages. Since 1970, death has accounted for less than half of all marital dissolutions annually; divorce now accounts for the majority of dissolutions. Theodore Kemper even argues that there are many reasons to suspect that divorce will actually decrease. Besides the demographic reasons that we have already noted (declining marriage rate, later marriage, more singles, and a slowdown in geographic mobility), he cites improved mental health, an upper limit to women's labor force participation, and a growing fear of the consequences of divorce. He also notes the end of postponed divorce now that no-fault divorce laws are well in place, the end of a cultural revolution stressing individualism exclusive of relationship, and the end of an unrealistic optimism about personal affluence. Furthermore, migration flow, which is correlated with age, will decline as the younger proportion decreases, and will probably follow the patterns already established between and within regions through the end of the century.[7]

These patterns also describe increasingly diverse experiences for young people outside the assumed normal family. One in four currently lives without both parents in the household, most often with the mother. During childhood, one in three white and two in three black children born after marriage can expect to experience loss of one parent by age sixteen.[8] While divorce rather than death almost always precipitates this situation, there are one in twenty who live with a never married mother and they represent a fourfold increase since 1970.[9] A recent study by Sandra Hofferth (1985) based on U.S. Census data and the twelve-year Panel Study on Income Dynamics (1968–1979) projects that for children born in 1980, 70 percent of whites and 94 percent of blacks will have spent at least some time with only *one* parent before they reach age eighteen in 1998.[10] Of course, the family into which a child is born greatly affects these chances. Yet for those children born into first-marriage two-parent families, 64 percent of whites and 89 percent of blacks can expect to spend time with only one parent. In fact, this will average about a quarter of the childhood for such whites and almost half (44 percent) of the childhood for such blacks. While these are only projections, they are based on the experiences of over 5,000 real families studied for more than a decade.

The growing proportion of single mothers highlights another social problem for such a modern society. Teenage pregnancy (1 in 10) and never married mothers are on the increase in the United States. Compared to other countries in the developed world, we have about twice the pregnancies for this age group and correspondingly poorer use of and access to contraceptives, particularly for first intercourse. This problem has several important dimensions for American families, including teenage sexual activity, out-of-wedlock childbearing, unintended pregnancy, and the lifelong consequences for parent and child of early pregnancy.

Here are some of the facts. Males are more sexually active than females (in 1979 a metropolitan U.S. study reported 77 percent versus 69 percent), yet the gap has diminished markedly in the last twenty years. Premarital sexual intercourse increases with age. Blacks are more active than whites (in 1982 for nineteen-year-old never married women, 81 percent versus 63 percent). "Between 1970 and 1982, the proportion of all births to women aged 15–19 that occurred out of wedlock rose from 17 to 37 percent among white women and from 62 to 87 percent among black women. The proportion of total births to all women under 20 that were out-of-wedlock was 51 percent in the U.S. in 1982."[11] Unintended pregnancies in 1978 accounted for 86 percent of the pregnancies that occurred to unmarried adolescents as well as 51 percent of married teenage pregnancy. The consequences for health, both physical and mental, of mother or child are serious. The social costs can also be very damaging, particularly as they affect education. "In the U.S., only 50 percent of teenage women who give birth before 18 ever complete high school, compared to 96 percent who do not have children before age 20. Teenage fathers are affected too, as only 70 percent complete high school, compared to 95 percent of nonparenting teen men."[12]

According to a recent Congressional Budget Office report from a Congressional Research Service study, 22.2 percent of all children in the United States now live in poverty.[13] This new high is one consequence of the two trends that are creating greater diversity within families—divorce and single parenthood. The female-headed families produced by these factors, in combination with the continued discrimination in women's wages, account for significant growth in poverty living for women and children. Women's employment is clearly the key to resolving the problem, while family planning and premarital and marriage counseling may serve to prevent it initially. Both of these are shorter-term tactics for battling the larger issue of sexism in our culture which produces these and many other social problems for families today. Though women are out in the labor force many more hours a week, their work at home remains great and unbalanced by husbands whose domestic contribution has only increased by minutes per week. Furthermore, as the family grows larger and work increases, the husband's participation actually decreases.[14]

The participation of women in the labor force has had the most dramatic impact on the family of any social force in our society today. A Rand Corporation study demonstrates that since 1960, these work factors—proportion of women employed and women's hourly wage—have had the most significant effect on the fertility rate, replacing the family income as a factor and minimizing explanations such as attitude change and the technological advances of the pill.[15] Of greater consequence to families is the displacement of one normative type of married couple household (male breadwinner, female housewife, and/or children) with another by at least 53 percent (dual-earner couple and/or children). Employed mothers are experienced by a majority of today's children, most recently for preschoolers with 52 percent in 1984, but ever since 1970 for those six and over reaching 65 percent in 1984.[16]

Before leaving the big picture, we need to examine two areas more closely for their impact on the family—migration and aging. The long-established frostbelt-to-sunbelt shift in growth, North to South and East to West, will continue but at a much reduced volume. Prime mover ages have peaked in the early 1980s. The complexity of the moving since 1970, particularly nonmetropolitan growth[17] and increasing suburbanization rates for blacks in large cities,[18] creates new patterns in communities across America. Energy resource industries, better transportation, and job availability fuel the first movement, while residential life quality encourages both. Neither trend removes the pressing urban problems of mostly nonwhite central cities. But the bloom is off much of Southern city growth, too, as overbuilding, growing unemployment, and traffic congestion plague urban life in the sunbelt.[19] The regional changes projected by the Census Bureau as reported by Family Service America[20] indicate that we are in the decade where rate of growth will increase slightly for the Northeast and the Midwest, while rate of growth will drop dramatically for the South and the West. The actual population growth changes remain much higher in the 1980s for the South (14.4 percent) and the West (13.4 percent) than for the Northeast (4.7 percent) and the Midwest (5.0 percent). The last decade of the century will see the least growth ever in the United States (6.8 percent)—even less than the decade of the Great Depression. The regional growth variation will also be reduced by the end of the century.

The changing age structure of America also deserves comment. As the baby boom cohort expands the middle-aged proportion, we will see fewer young and preretirement adults, a constant fraction of children (around 25 percent), and more elderly. We will particularly see more of the old old —over seventy-five or eighty. This age group has much greater health care needs; and, while the number institutionalized may never exceed the current 5 percent or less of those over sixty-five, many will be making increasing demands on younger generations in their own families and social services within their communities. A 1975 study estimated that 15 percent of the elderly have chronic conditions that require regular assistance to maintain themselves in the community.[21] This is especially problematic for middle-aged women whose increasing labor force participation and previous migration make them less able and less available to provide such care to older parents, aunts, and uncles without major disruptions to their life. Many of the care givers are elderly themselves, and less capable of providing such stress-inducing assistance. As government continues to cut back at the federal level, this problem may become particularly acute in many regions of the country. For example, in the Northeast and the Midwest elderly have been left by younger outmigration, and in the South local government services have many pressing demands from recent growth and may give much less priority to the older population. The smaller family of recent decades further exacerbates this problem for many people, since the burden will be shared by even fewer persons.

A CHURCH EXAMPLE—PRESBYTERIAN DEMOGRAPHY

In looking at the patterns of change in one denomination, we utilized the 1984 Simmons report on The American Presbyterian and also the fourth generation of the Panel of the former United Presbyterian Church U.S.A. compiled in early 1982, along with some information from previous rounds that provide us with trend information.[22] The main purpose is better use of national information in the light of some characteristics unique to Presbyterians.

The age and sex structure looks a lot the way America will look in another fifty years or so. We still have disproportionately more females as members (the proportion of females with self-declared Presbyterian identity is equivalent to the U.S. population at 53 percent) and fewer young adults, but a basically stable and perhaps stationary age and sex structure for the adult membership. (This structure is so unlike a pyramid that its graphic depiction almost replicates the silhouette of Chimney Rock at Ghost Ranch, New Mexico—that is, with a wider top half than bottom half!) The leadership is still dominated by men, particularly at the staff/clergy level, and in the new Presbyterian Church (U.S.A.) the male elders are probably in greater proportion than was true of the former United Presbyterian Church U.S.A., where they were 60 percent. Given the greater affluence of Presbyterians compared to the nation as a whole, they can be a setting for an effective model of older community organization—the future of America. An interesting discrepancy between laity and clergy comes with age comparisons as the laity reflect this future stable age structure and the clergy reflect America's current baby boom bulge of young adults. This has major implications for projecting professional needs and candidate committee work. On the local scene it also suggests an asynchrony between membership life-style and clergy family life.

The small young adult proportion raises concern with many but ought to be balanced with an understanding of the qualities of this stage of life that mitigate against church membership. Disruptions come from pursuit of education, job search and early career mobility, dual earner couples' competing demands, and later marriage and family starts. It should also be noted that fewer in this age bracket may participate in a Panel study that requires a three-year commitment when even next year's prospects are unknown.

The racial homogeneity of Presbyterians stands in stark contrast to the sizable minority groups of the United States. Blacks are only 2 percent of Presbyterians versus 12 percent nationally, and Hispanics are less than 1 percent versus 6 percent nationally. This lack of diversity at all levels may inhibit understanding and respect for the ways that families differ across many areas addressed in this chapter—marital status, fertility, residential location, and others.

It appears that Presbyterians characterize their communities as less urban than the average American. There was a rural growth in membership which paralleled that of nonmetropolitan growth in the nation in the 1970s, for the West and particularly for the Northeast, where the United Presbyterian Church U.S.A. had its largest representations. The South and the Midwest have seen greater metropolitan membership, with recent growth for the sunbelt given the national trends. On the whole, these may balance others in differentiating change by community type since 1970.

In areas of family life (marital status and household composition) as well as socioeconomic status (education, income, and occupation), Presbyterians are not typical of the nation. While showing that slightly more are married, the 1982 Panel indicated that a two-thirds (65 percent) majority lives without children present compared with just less than half (46 percent) of the U.S. population (see graph). Because of the older age structure, many Presbyterians have children who have grown and gone. In contrast, their pastors are more likely to have children present (65 percent). Elders are in between, closer to the general membership with a smaller majority (59 percent) without children present. There are fewer divorced members and more widowed members in comparison to the nation as a whole—another future related to our older age structure. There has been less changing in family status areas because of this older and stabler age structure in the past decade.

In socioeconomic terms, Presbyterians have always been above average in the U.S. population. Their strong emphasis on education leads to much more professional and managerial work and concomitant higher income. For males, this means that 40 percent (versus 16 percent U.S.) hold proprietor or managerial positions. For females, there are more striking differences in professional attainment (52 percent versus 17 percent U.S.) and only minor administrative advantage (11 percent versus 7 percent U.S.). The remaining 37 percent of each sex work in other occupations—about half the national average in other occupations for males (70 percent) and for females (76 percent). It is interesting that though a significant 25 percent of the male members are now retired, female members are working more but are "somewhat less likely than other American women to be either 'homemakers' or employed full-time, and somewhat more likely to be employed on a part-time basis or retired."[23] Clergy wives have increased their labor force participation

Percentages of Presbyterian Families at Various Stages

Family Stage	Members	Elders	Pastors	Specialized*
Teenage children	10	14	15	18
Children ages 6 to 12	12	15	18	14
Preschool children	12	12	22	14
No children born	19	12		9
			12	
All children grown	47	47	33	45

*Specialized clergy in United Presbyterian Church—related ministries.

SOURCE: Adapted from Figure 7, *The Presbyterians: A Background Report on Those Who Constitute the Panel and on the Reestablishment of the Panel* (New York: Research Unit, Support Agency, United Presbyterian Church U.S.A., 1982), p. 20.

significantly in recent years with corresponding enhancement of clergy family income.

The income picture for Presbyterians, while well above national figures, does actually represent a slightly diminished purchasing power, according to the 1982 Panel. Again, an older age structure, with its reduced income of retirees and widows, plays an important part in differentiating Presbyterians from typical Americans. About half of all members live in dual-earner families now; however, 70 percent of those with household income under $15,000 have only one wage earner.

Before we leave the Panel data, it seems appropriate to note two findings. One finding concerns friendships, church attendance, and the proportion of close friends within the congregation. The other describes political orientation in various segments. With the increasing diversity of households in the United States and growth in the number of persons who live alone, it seems important to point out that having close friendships within a congregation doubles the probability of members' worship participation from 30 to 62 percent a month. With the political conservatism of the decade, it also seems important to recognize the diversity of political opinion within the church. The clergy are more moderate to liberal, while the laity are more conservative to moderate. But within the laity, men are more conservative and women are more liberal.[24] The findings have significant implications for overcoming some of the homogeneity of family status among Presbyterians and for exercising caution in program development through critical participation to assure proper representation.

RESPONSIBLE EXPECTATIONS AND ACTIONS

Family ministry needs to diversify. The large intact number of families of the midcentury which brought focused demands in Christian education and youth programs has yielded to the four varieties that we currently see, in different proportions, among Presbyterians and in the nation.

These four family types are the older couple, the two-parent family, the single-parent family, and the young couple. One could also make a good argument for defining the single individual as a fifth family type, characterized by no immediate residential relationships. Let us take each of these in turn and consider how the church can minister to them.

The Older Couple

The older couple is the dominant family of the laity. Most older couples have children who are grown and gone. While it is typical of only a third of local pastors, most specialized clergy (executive staff, for example) also live without children present. With this type in the majority, the church needs a strategy that enriches adult education, renews leadership, sustains commitment, and develops programming for aging members. Marriage enrichment is important always, but especially after child launching. The older couple may have spent years busy in separate arenas—the business world and the domestic scene—with the child-related responsibilities serving to keep connections on a regular basis. Now that their children are gone, the opportunity to revitalize the marriage may need positive action so that the couple do not grow farther apart by merely maintaining separate activities. The anticipation of changes facing such couples can create content for part of such efforts. Thinking toward new relationships in the community as death results in lost relationships requires obvious faith perspective. Other changes would also benefit from careful consideration within the church. Retirement, grandparenthood, chronic illness, coping with aged parents, residential moves, all affect the meaning of people's lives. The church can assist the later lives of its members by responding with ceremony, sponsoring self-help groups, and initiating study for planning. Coordinating the talents of others in the church who can give relief and reassurance to persons under particular stress is an important nurturing function. The church has lost some of its power to act in such capacities where unicameral boards have replaced deacons and where women's organizations have lost the volunteer hours available in earlier periods when fewer women were employed.

The contribution of the older couple in ministry to others in the church should not be neglected. One strategy for tapping this resource would pair older with younger in committee work or classroom teaching responsibilities. For some this may combine experience with energy, for others a steady presence with one drawn away occasionally by work demands. The mobility of younger families can create a generation contact loss unless churches encourage the adoption of church grandparents as well as more homogeneous age groupings.

The older couple can be the backbone of the church's ministry to the very aged. Visits, meals brought to homes, respite care, phone calls, hospice work, and assistance with participation for worship and other church events are crucial ministries that require time and care. Transportation supplied when one is able establishes a model that later may assure one of rides when one becomes aged. Such exchange is celebrated in a local congregation that cultivates time and talent dimensions of stewardship along with the financial. The older couples' time contributions balance the younger members' economic contributions.

To the degree that local clergy life-style is younger, presbyteries and older pastors may assist congregations in reviewing the older family ministry efforts. Seminaries are beginning to educate about aging, but experience and participation should not be wasted resources within the church. In a very important way, Presbyterians now have the composition of America's future, but with the advantage of some extra resources to cope with all the ramifications involved. Our present organizational health is largely attributable to the past participation of older members and their continuing contributions. We provide a good example to dispel one of the worst myths of aging: old age is *not* a dismal and unproductive existence. We need to be advocates in the larger community as well as models for assisting effective, long, full, and independent living in old age. Caring for our own and reaching out to others in coordination with community service agencies is already a feature more typical of Presbyterians than of average Americans. The aging society around us is a critical focus for these volunteer impulses in the future.

The Two-Parent Family

The second family type—that of the two-parent family with children present—is not the same one we have dealt with in the past. At least two major developments have altered its complexion and now challenge us to more responsive ministry. These developments are women's increasing labor force participation and the growing number of reconstituted families with new and complicated relationships.

The family with dual earners and young children is under considerable stress. While many have conceived of this as self-imposed, few who analyze the economic reality for families today would define women's employment as a matter of choice. As working-class women have long known and middle-class women are now finding out, employment is a necessity for a significant part of adult life.

This situation should be accepted as we review its many ramifications for the church. The first concern is that of appropriate expectations for women's participation in the church. With work time impinging on their household activities, women have already particularly full days. Therefore, their volunteer involvements become very limited. The changing nature of the activity of women in women's organizations of the church and the increased burden on some who can continue to supply food, decorations, and arrangements for various church functions as well as new participation in leadership—elders, clergy, and seminarians—reflect the revolution in the outside world. Rather than bemoaning the lost days of women's programs in the past, congregations should be preparing all of their membership to make contributions as they can. The increased population of single young adults is certainly demonstrating that males can adequately perform domestic tasks formerly left to women and that women can assist with maintenance areas formerly left to men. Employed men have long juggled church and job, but with a wife to handle much of the domestic scene. Churches can encourage the more egalitarian attitude of today's parents in avoiding a one-sex gender bias *and* alternating demands on parents to allow their balancing of family demands with full church participation. The local congregation can review who should be asked to help in the kitchen and who should be asked to serve on presbytery committees.

Dual-earner families need endorsement as legitimate models for nurturing human relationships and faith within the church. Christian education materials and youth socialization should emphasize the employment experience in everyone's future and a team approach to domestic tasks. In raising these concerns, the church is not neglecting or diminishing the breadwinner/homemaker family model but is advocating God's action in multiple-family forms with different needs and contributions. This kind of realism is as important for boys as it is for girls. Such dual-earner families have greater need for open communication and coordination which are grounded in conveying earlier and more realistically the expectations about family living in general.

We cannot leave this aspect of two-parent families without discussing the child care industry in America. Churches have offered a crucial service in quality day care and after-school care and should continue to improve their own contribution and advocate for quality in all the community's child care services. Our physical plants can be, or truly have been, born again five times a week by this use of space and care of children. Whether or not a program explicitly involves Christian education should be less crucial than its quality of care for children and service to the community. Whether they are church-sponsored or separately incorporated, day care programs are vital to families and communities, and demand our close alliance to protect and nurture the young.

If any families are in need of recognition in today's world, then surely the reconstituted family deserves first billing.

While specialized ministry to divorced spouses and their children is clearly important in the period of crisis, the wider recognition and acceptance in the general life of the church seems missing. While we wouldn't advocate armbands for visibility or any stigmatizing treatment, we can celebrate new relationships and re-created families as special and requiring more covenanting than the first marriage situation. Perhaps "single again" ceremonies or stepchild adoptings or other appropriate rituals can affirm our faith, our struggle against sin, and our renewed attempts at committed life as partners in the family and in the life of the church.

Understanding time in reconstituted families is essential to youth programs and general weekend participation expectations for all family members. Multiple relationships demand time to preserve them, and these compete with typical church time. Those who can't be part of everything shouldn't be left behind. Those with changing transportation and resources shouldn't be forgotten. The church is challenged to rethink the issue of time and to try new uses of weekday opportunities or special but biweekly Sunday programs. Family-oriented vacation Bible school in early evening at midweek, or worship that moves to the end of the weekend to facilitate other outings, may be the only way some can participate in the life of the church. (We may discover that in trying to accommodate the special time dilemmas of reconstituted families, other ones—dual *career* families, those with split hours, and those with shift work—can again participate in the body of Christ.) Reconstituted families also have important ramifications for our older couples coping with redefined generational ties and having little recourse to maintain some relationships without good mediation and support from the church.

The One-Parent Family

One-parent families involve many of these new features of two-parent families, but with the disadvantage of diminished resources and time to do what needs to be done to live and

grow. Day care is even more critical for these families, though
that doesn't undermine the essential contribution of a mother's-day-out feature for homemakers in the same program.

Resource limits, time pressures, and relationship needs
characterize single-parent families. The church can respond
with appropriate expectations, flexibility, and open invitations. Special ministry of coordinating activities and nurturing individuals in the church family seems warranted.
Premarital counseling should deal realistically with the importance of commitment and the differential impact of broken commitments for the women of such situations. In our
nation many are projecting that most children will spend
some time in one-parent families.[25] We must be prepared to
maintain relationships with individuals while they are
changing relationships with each other.

In our larger ministry to such families we must respond
to the feminization of poverty and the rising levels of children raised in such conditions. Present trends project that
few men will be classified in poverty by the turn of the
century—only women, the young with dependent children,
and the growing proportion of widows and the old. The minority representation would be inexcusable to a modern-day
Jeremiah or Amos. Where is the justice?

The Young Couple

The fourth family type is not well represented in the Presbyterian Church. Young couples without children, perhaps
never expecting to have any (and possibly without marriage
to define the relationship), are probably much fewer than the
9 to 19 percent noted in the 1982 Panel as "no children born
to family." Several of these could be older childless couples.
The slight fraction who might be cohabiting are more than
likely part of the well-educated later-to-marry type described by Cherlin.[26] While the church may not wish to sanction such arrangements, it should recognize this new stage
of adult relationships as perhaps more probable, particularly for Americans of higher status. Many European coun-

tries see this as the majority practice today. Our approach might be more effective if we were genuinely interested in the covenant dimensions of this nonmarital relationship. Housing availability, economic resources, and life-style changes (such as later marriage and independent living) all encourage innovations. Group arrangements offer communal ties which are important to young adults today—much as they were to early Christians.

The mobility of young couples, while it may interfere with community involvement, should not prevent the church from reaching out. With the increasing proportion of young singles who live alone, effective programming for this age group (those with or without family and dependents) may be an appropriate avenue to enrich the church with young adult participation. The friendship relation to attendance in congregations should extend beyond marital or family similarity for the young adults. Early extension of leadership opportunities also seems important for developing skills and resources among them. Churches in college and university communities that are not reaching out to the campuses are missing an important resource for youth programs, infusion of new ideas, and cultivating leadership. While the arrival of children may have precipitated church involvement in past generations, Presbyterians in today's world should consider other avenues for fulfilling the needs of young adults. They need the age-integrated church family as much as our age structure needs them and the renewal they bring. Faith questions are of growing importance to the baby bust generation. (Baby bust refers to those born from 1960 through 1974, when fertility rates were dropping fast from the baby boom peak in 1957.) And the nation's swing toward more conservatism should provide an easier mesh with general political orientation of Presbyterian laity.

The Single-Member Family

Single individuals deserve attention as a family type for two reasons. First, the younger ones are, in most cases, seeking relationships rather than rejecting them. Second, the older ones have many family roles—for example, widow, grandparent, sibling, aunt—that define their lives and lifestyles in significant ways despite the missing domestic component. Both offer family forces for our faith community which spill over to enrich those still residing in families. Chronicling their contribution seems an appropriate enterprise for consciousness-raising as we think about faith and families in the church. These "families" offer the greatest variety within any type considered here and thus present the greatest challenge to our ministry.

CONCLUSION

Though the church is made up of individuals, their identity is shaped by families in the church, the community, the nation, and the world. In identifying five types of families, we have noted many variations. We hope these will continue to add to the church and its complexity in the future.

In a consideration of the merits of age-segregated versus age-integrated programming for any type of family, many issues could be raised. The most critical factor in planning ministry with families is probably size of congregation. On the one hand, large churches can afford extensive age and family type programming. However, they risk the fragmentation that defeats one of the most unique features of the church. In the world today, the church is the most age-integrated institution. On the other hand, small churches risk satisfying no one's needs if every activity is age integrated. However, they may not have the critical mass necessary for some age and family type of specific programs. The intergenerational nature of the church is one of its best mechanisms for accommodating the diverse and complex experience of families. The balance of age and family type of activities with whole church programs needs special attention in every congregation and by every level of our church organization.

Families are more diversified and more complicated. They

still need faith and opportunities to demonstrate faith. Will the church respond in sufficient diversity and complexity to affirm the faith that families require? Will the families so nurtured respond in faith in the world? Our society can only benefit if we renew that faith and challenge our communities to the new understanding of family life today.

3

Resilient Families, Competencies, Supports, and Coping Over the Life Cycle

Hamilton I. McCubbin and Marilyn A. McCubbin

As a developing society, we are moving into a restructuring phase characterized by shifting norms. We are part of an economy based on the creation and distribution of information, and propelled by an explosion of high technology complemented by a compensatory human response. There is a shift from institutionalized help to more self-reliance and emphasis upon informal networks. We are becoming a free-wheeling multiple-option society. Caught in such rapid and profound change, families are experiencing turbulence. Amid a painful and ambiguous present, the restructuring and adaptation of American families are also taking place.

In order to understand families in this situation, social scientists have attempted to take snapshots of American families in transition. One picture of American families portrayed in the literature today is that of a disturbed and struggling social organization characterized by divorces, remarriages, single-parent households, alternative life-styles, same-sex partners in raising children, delayed marriages, parenthood in later years, and two-parent households. One could argue that the emergence of alternative structures and changing patterns in family relationships reflects a

The project on which this chapter was based was supported by the Graduate School, Wisconsin Alumni Research Foundation, University of Wisconsin, Madison, Wisconsin.

questionable response to the "high-tech, high-touch" character of the 1980s. Families are falling apart, some may lament.

As social scientists, we would argue against this limited understanding of families in an era of social change. Family social scientists have tried to probe more deeply in an effort to understand the family processes involved in adaptation to change. Through research we have discovered the *positive interpersonal processes of family adaptation* to stress and change. Family researchers have seized the unique opportunity presented by today's changes to determine what makes resilient families—social units that not only are capable of adapting but that thrive in the context of turbulence and stress. This line of scientific study is based on the belief that family adaptation to change is facilitated by specific intrafamily competencies, coping skills, interpersonal resources, and community supports. If we understand these processes, we will be in a better position to help families help themselves and become more self-reliant.

Adversity brings out the vulnerabilities and strengths in families. Guided by the Chinese perspective that "crises present both danger and opportunity," we believe that research on families struggling with change has shed light upon what makes families survive and function in the face of adversity. Such research also has the potential of advancing our understanding of the hardiness in families, those characteristics of family life which allow them to develop and mature despite the many hardships they face. This chapter focuses on family resiliency in the face of extreme hardships—the coping repertoires that families employ, the interpersonal resources they call upon and develop, the internal competencies they develop and maintain, and their transactions with the community to obtain strengths.

RESILIENCY IN THE FACE OF CHANGE

In order to highlight the importance of resilience in families, we need to focus on the dynamics of family adaptation.[1]

We assume that in the face of stressors and crises, families will struggle to adapt. That is, they will seek a satisfactory level of functioning in which family members *(a)* work to be supportive of each other and achieve a "fit" among persons in the unit; *(b)* work together to promote both togetherness and independence; *(c)* are encouraged to develop strong personalities, skills, and abilities that will put them in a positive position for managing the future on their own; and *(d)* achieve a satisfactory and mutually supportive "fit" in the community in which they reside.[2] This is a difficult challenge for even the best of families.

Therefore family adaptation usually has a price tag. Unfortunately it may be a long time before we actually know the outcome of family efforts to cope with the stressors and strains of life in the process of change. We need to be concerned. Men and women have physiological and psychological endowments, and families have certain capabilities that give adaptive potential in the face of extremely unfavorable conditions. However, the fact that all subsequent aspects of personal and family life are affected by what came before makes such adaptation a double-edged sword. Evaluated over the entire life span, the homeostatic mechanisms through which family adaptation is achieved often fail in the long run because they result in delayed pathological effects.

Adaptation is obviously an asset for survival and seems to assure the continued interpersonal success of family life. Paradoxically, the very fact that families readily achieve sociocultural adjustments to so many different kinds of stresses and undesirable conditions is dangerous for its welfare and possibly its future. Many of the health problems of modern America have their origin in the slowly developing injurious effects of the technological environment and the new ways of life. Children, for example, can learn to adapt to social stressors by seeking happiness through overeating, unsuitable amusements, and perverted addictions. Adults may experience stressors the effects of which become inscribed in the body and the mind without the affected person's realizing that he or she is being changed irreversibly by influences that do not enter the consciousness. Adaptations to environmental and interpersonal threats are often achieved through a blunting of awareness and can thereby interfere with the recognition and appreciation of human values. The quality of human relationships can degenerate under stress without the persons involved being conscious of the loss this entails. René Dubos[3] called attention to one of the worst consequences of modern life—the *autonomy-with-drawal syndrome.* Most people, he claims, use their homes to escape from the stresses of the outside world and practice social withdrawal as a form of self-protection. Extreme individualism and autonomy commonly develop unconsciously as a consequence of the self-protective withdrawal from stress. Families are called upon to absorb and buffer the burdens of members seeking to escape from the stressors and strains of this high-tech society. Obviously there are limits to how much present families can absorb and manage.

THE HAWAIIAN FAMILY IN MODERN AMERICA—A CASE IN POINT

A congressional commission was asked to study the children in Hawaii[4] to determine the generational effects of Westernization and cultural adaptation. Overall, Hawaii ranks second in health and first in environmental quality of life. The early Hawaiians lived in a community and family in which an orderly system of status, responsibilities, and relationships prevailed. A clearly defined hierarchy existed. No attempt was made to dominate the land, or the plants and animals therein; rather, there was a deep respect for the environment and an emphasis on living in harmony with nature. No one threw trash into the streams or the sea, or dirtied the earth. The lesson remembered was that everything is a gift and everything should be shared. Family consciousness was a unifying and deeply felt force among the Hawaiians. Ohana, the family clan or extended family, is derived from the oha, the root of the taro plant (the staple of the Hawaiian diet), and signifies the same root of origin for its members. Senior members were respected. The Hawaiians thus had a clear sense of their link and place in time and received emotional supports from spiritual ancestors as well as earthly members of the family. Children were cherished in the Hawaiian culture.

This all changed with Captain Cook and with statehood. Hawaii evolved into a multiethnic, modern society with all its attendant advantages and disadvantages—instant communication with the rest of the world, high rises, daily jets, superhighways, and fast food. Hawaiians placed great emphasis upon human relationships. Aggressive, challenging, and confrontative behaviors were avoided, or were undertaken at the risk of personal anxiety and group censure. The charting of new identities and life-styles with confusing directional markers was not without much pain and anguish and, for some, failure. The congressional commission found that the price of Hawaiian family adaptation to the many changes was high.

- The Hawaiian / part-Hawaiian ethnic group had the highest or next highest rate for all health indices studied except for tuberculosis and cerebrovascular disease.
- The Hawaiian / part-Hawaiian ethnic group has the highest teenage pregnancy rate—followed closely by the Samoan and Filipino groups. The levels are double the rate for Caucasians and triple the rates for Japanese and Chinese.
- Confirmed cases of child abuse and neglect are disproportionately high for Hawaiian children.
- Hawaiians are more than half of the population of the youth correction facility, almost half of the residents in adult correctional facilities, and a high percentage of those on parole. They also lead all other ethnic groups in serious crimes committed and arrests in proportion to their percentage of the population.
- Hawaiians are disproportionately represented among school dropouts, among those with an excessive number of absences from school, and in truancy statistics.

Unfortunately we have cultivated the myth that the family has an infinite capacity to adapt to changing environments and that we can endlessly and safely transform its structure and indeed its internal processes. In reality there are social and psychological limits to family adaptation, and these should determine the frontiers of technological change. But we do not know precisely what these limits are. What major family characteristics—particularly strengths, competencies, coping strategies, and supports—buffer these families from the impact of stressors and strains? However, in an effort to advance this line of scientific inquiry, and to call attention to the resiliency in families, it would be useful to look at extant studies of family responses to crises, and differences in family responses across the stages of the family life cycle.

Situational Crises: Identifying Critical Competencies, Supports, and Coping

Investigators associated with the Family Stress and Coping Project[5] have now accumulated information about family adaptation to major situational crises. It has been twelve years since the return of American prisoners of war from Vietnam and our research on family adaptation following the French Indochina War, ten years since our collaborative work with the Israeli military in Jerusalem regarding family adaptation to the hardships of the Yom Kippur War, and thirteen years since we began to work with Regents Professor Reuben Hill in the advancement of research on families under stress. What have we found?

Prolonged War-induced Crisis: Family Adaptation

It has been ten years since we began the longitudinal study of 216 families who faced the adversity of coping with a missing member—husbands and fathers who had been absent for an average of 6.6 years, or who remain unaccounted for in the Vietnam War.[6] In this research, we learned about the importance of the following:

Maintaining family integrity—behavior directed toward keeping the family unit together as a cohesive unit, particularly in the face of an ambiguous situation where the outcome seemed unclear.

Developing social support—behavior directed toward developing and maintaining meaningful relationships outside the family unit which gave the family a sense of being valued and appreciated.

Developing self-reliance—behavior directed toward developing personal skills and abilities, personal strengths, and independence for family members, which in turn facilitated their management of the present difficulties and preparation for an uncertain future.

Collective group supports—involvement of families, banding together in a collective unit to change the governmental policies and programs that appeared to impede their adaptation and to institute more supportive policies and programs.

Developing a shared meaning, a sense of coherence—behavior directed toward developing within the family unit a shared understanding, trust and acceptance, usually with the assistance of their spiritual beliefs, thus making the difficulties comprehensible and meaningful.

Families were extremely powerful, particularly when they banded together in an effort to alter existing policies so as to support families. Never in the history of the American military had we witnessed what constructive family power can do. New policies were established to give families more autonomy, more control, and more resources needed to cope with the unfortunate circumstance. The National League of Families pushed Congress and the Department of Defense to give female spouses freedom to act on behalf of their families, in the absence of the military member. This was a very significant step forward in developing the rights of women in the military context.

Coherence[7] or shared meaning was particularly important to these families struggling to give meaning to long years of waiting with the likely possibility that their significant member was not to return. Shared meaning helped the family pull together and face the future from a position of strength. One family comes to mind as an example of efforts to develop this important sense of coherence.

Mrs. Johnson was the spouse of a Navy navigator who was shot down over Vietnam. After six years of waiting with little hope, she attempted to get on with her life and to move the family, which included her son Steve, forward in a new life-style on a Wisconsin farm. She completed her bachelor's degree, started graduate studies, and built her own home. She also established a farm, where she planned to rear her son. But Steve believed that his father would return and resisted any attempts to close out his father's role in the family. Predictably, this curtailed Mrs. Johnson's efforts to establish meaningful relationships and the prospects of a remarriage. The Johnson family did not develop a shared definition of the situation.

This was changed, however, in a very special situation. We had the good fortune of working with these families during a family religious retreat in the Colorado Rockies. Those of us who conducted the longitudinal studies knew these families well. One sunny day, while on a walk with Mrs. Johnson and Steve, I was struck by Steve's personal revelation. On the walk, he stared at a tall dead pine tree that had just a few branches, without any foliage. "That is my dad. He is dead, you know. He died in a plane crash in Vietnam. He really won't return, you know." Turning his attention to a little sapling, a little developing tree, just at the base of the tall dead pine, Steve commented with tears in his eyes: "I am that little tree. You see, my dad died so that I could grow and become a man." The bright sun shone down upon this little tree, as Mrs. Johnson tried to hold back her tears, without success.

Family Routine Crises:
Family Adaptation

It has been six years since we conducted one of the first prospective studies of military families experiencing the stressor of a military member at sea for nine months. We interviewed families before, during, and following the separation, and we studied fathers while they were at sea.[8] This unique study of eighty-two families called our attention to the importance of the following:

Maintaining family integrity—behavior directed toward keeping the family unit together as a cohesive unit.

Developing self-reliance and self-esteem—behavior directed toward developing personal skills, abilities, and strengths, and toward becoming involved in activities (e.g., work, volunteer programs, education) designed to enhance the sense of well-being and worth.

Androgynous gender-role orientation—perception of self as being endowed with both masculine and feminine values, attitudes, and behavior—expressive, communal, as well as instrumental and agenital.

Developing and maintaining social support—behavior directed toward developing and maintaining meaningful relationships outside the family unit which gave the family members a sense of being valued and appreciated.

Developing family competencies and strengths—efforts to prepare the family in advance for the separation by having a legal will prepared, getting a power of attorney, communication with each other about feelings and concerns, and planning for various problems and their solutions.

Family competencies and strengths, particularly marital communication, complemented by social support, appeared to work as buffers against the hardships associated with the separation. Families who felt a part of and were involved in the community and who had meaningful friendships were better able to endure the situational hardships.

Spouses who had an androgynous gender-role orientation (i.e., the capability of responding with positive masculine and feminine characteristics such as caring and assertiveness)[9] appeared to have a broader coping repertoire. They were adept at *(a)* keeping the family functioning as a cohesive unit; *(b)* maintaining a high level of emotional and esteem support; *(c)* keeping tension low and under control; *(d)* and accepting the demands of the military life-style. It was not surprising that spouses who saw themselves as having both instrumental and expressive characteristics appeared to have more flexibility in responding to the diverse demands of the situation created by the separation. They could draw on a broad range of behavioral responses designed to attend to a range of family needs.

Chronically Ill Children and Chronic Crises: Family Adaptation

It has been four years since we began three major studies of families with chronically ill children—families who had children with cystic fibrosis, with cerebral palsy, and with myelomeningocele. We initiated our research on the association between family functioning, parental coping, and social support in such crises and developmental and physiological changes in these chronically ill children (e.g., pulmonary functioning laboratory tests, height and weight, and health status). It has been a relatively brief period since we began our collaborative work with physicians, family practitioners, and nurses.[10] The critical coping strategies, family strengths, and competencies were the following:

Family integration—The mother's and father's coping efforts to keep the family together and maintain an optimistic outlook were important in promoting the child's health.

Support and esteem—The mother's coping efforts to get support and to develop her esteem and self-confidence were important in promoting the child's health. The father's coping efforts to get support and to develop his self-esteem and self-confidence were important in promoting the child's health.

Family functioning—The family's active orientation toward participating in various recreational and sporting activities was positively associated with improvements in the child's health. The findings also indicated that the greater the family's emphasis on control and family organization, rules, and procedures, the greater the improvement in the child's health.

Family mastery and health—The family's efforts to maintain a sense of order and optimism and the health of all family members were positively related to improvements in the chronically ill child's health status, and negatively related to the number of active health problems these children may have.

TRANSITIONAL CRISES OVER THE LIFE CYCLE: IDENTIFYING CRITICAL COMPETENCIES, SUPPORTS, AND COPING

A family's strengths and competencies can vary across the family life cycle, particularly in relationship to the age of the children and the social situation in which families place themselves (e.g., entering and exiting from the work force, advancing in the work setting). The research team, therefore, also examined which family strengths, competencies, coping skills, and social supports are important for families at the various stages of the family life cycle. Two major family surveys were conducted: one focusing upon normal (nonclinic) families (1,000 families), and another on military families (1,000) relocated to a foreign country and placed in a high-stress, high-risk situation along the East German and Czechoslovakian borders.

Family Stress and Strengths Over the Life Cycle: Family Adaptation

It has been two years since the completion of our collaborative work on a national survey of 1,000 families—their stressors, strains, strengths, coping, and support[11] (see Figure 1).

All families encounter stress. But does the amount of

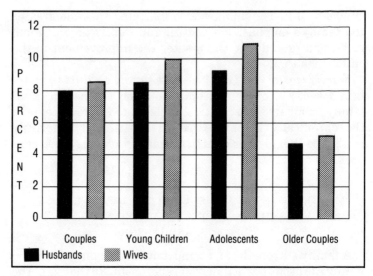

Figure 1. Percent of Families Indicating High Stress at Stages of Family Life Cycle

stress change as a family matures over the life cycle? And does the amount of stress vary between family members in the same family unit? As might be expected, the number of stressors and strains increased during much of the life cycle, reaching the highest point when there were adolescents in the home (see Figure 1). Stress levels dropped to the lowest point when the couples were older and the children had transitioned from the home. The difference in stressors and strains that husbands and wives experienced appeared directly related to there being children, adolescents, or young adults in the home. Early in a marriage and during the empty nest and retirement years, when there were no children in the household, the husband and wife reported nearly identical levels of stress. The parenting years (preschool, school age, and adolescent) and launching years not only were more demanding but also were periods in which husbands and wives were most likely to differ in the hardships they experience and record.

Family strength and competencies were also recorded and varied across stages of the family life cycle.

Resilient young couples were characterized as having family accord (low conflict), a satisfying marital communication, personality compatibility, agreement on finances, and enjoyable leisure.

Resilient families with young children were characterized as having family accord (low conflict), a satisfying marital communication, good relationships with family and friends, agreement on finances, enjoyment of children, family satisfaction, and life satisfaction.

Resilient families with adolescents were characterized as having personality compatibility, good relationships with family and friends, agreement on finances, satisfying sexual relationship, marriage satisfaction, and life satisfaction.

Resilient older couples were characterized as having satisfying marital communication and personality compatibility.

Family resistance to stress and recovery from distress may well be facilitated, in part, by family strengths, coping, and resources. The importance and critical nature of specific family and social resources vary according to the stage of the family life cycle and the demands unique to each stage of family development. A summary of the most important resources characteristic of low-stress families at each stage is given in Figure 2.

To identify the critical resources that help families deal with stress, couple and family strengths were explored at each stage. The major resource that seemed to distinguish those who coped well with stress from those who coped poorly was feeling good about their marriage. This included satisfaction with marital communication, personality compatibility, good relationships with the spouse's family and friends, agreement on finances, and generally enjoyment of marriage. In addition, as indicated in Figure 3, spiritual support was a vital, if not critical, factor in the family's coping with stress.

	Couples	Preschool/School-age	Adolescents	Older/Retired
Family accord	◯	◯		
Satisfying marital communication	◯	◯		
Personality compatibility	◯		◯	◯
Good relations with family and friends		◯	◯	
Agreement on finances	◯	◯	◯	
Enjoyable leisure	◯			
Enjoyment of children		◯		
Satisfying sexual relationship			◯	
Family Life Cycle Stage	Couples	Preschool/School-age	Adolescents	Older/Retired

Figure 2. Critical Strengths Across Stages of Family Life Cycle

Families in High-Risk Environments: Family Adaptation from a Life-Cycle Perspective

It has been fifteen months since we completed the first major investigation of over 1,000 Army families in high-risk environments in West Germany, and particularly along the East German and Czechoslovakian borders. It has also been just a few months since we completed our negotiations with the Department of the Army to advance the publication of the results about resilient families in the Army. It has been but a few months since we began the first major investigation about the resilient characteristics of black families in the enlisted ranks of the Army.[12] The major findings (see Figure 4) associated with families of enlisted personnel in the Army are the following:

Resilient families in the couple stage were characterized as taking advantage of family time together, having spouses with coping skills for survival, having and promoting esteem support, living in a supportive community that cares about them, and having a meaningful job in the military.

Resilient families with preschool-age children were characterized as families in which both the husband and the wife had a strong sense of coherence (i.e., optimism, predictability, manageability, and trust), spouses were self-reliant, maintained continuity in employment status, took advantage of family time together, had social support from the community, and had less residual stress from leaving friends and relatives.

Resilient families with school-age children were characterized as having a strong sense of coherence (i.e., optimism, predictability, manageability, and trust) and as having and promoting esteem support; spouses were self-reliant and had coping skills for survival in West Germany (e.g., knowledge of language, use of transportation); such families had quality of family life, and fewer difficulties or hassles when they first arrived in the foreign country.

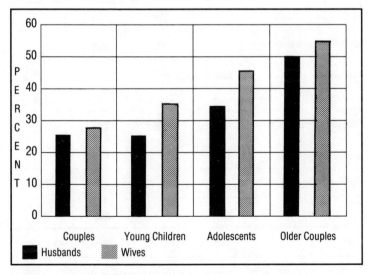

Figure 3. Percent Indicating Use of Spiritual Support to Cope with Stress

Resilient families in the adolescent and launching stage were characterized as having family esteem support, mutual emotional support for husband and wife, and quality of family life; they took advantage of family time together and shared roles in the family; and they had sponsorship support from the military community. Of added importance, these families had quality religious programs to facilitate their adaptation.

In general, these resilient families had developed or worked at developing internal strengths and capabilities, cultivated a shared sense of coherence about who they were and how they fit into the military community and its lifestyle, and seized available community supports, such as sponsors, religious programs, and friendships in the community, to help their adaptation.

	Couple	Preschool	School-age	Adolescent
Family time together	■	■		■
Soldier coherence-fit		■	■	
Spouse coherence-fit		■	■	
Support from friends	■	■		■
Spiritual support				■
Spouse self-reliance		■	■	
Spouse coping skills	■		■	
Family emotional support				■
Family esteem support	■		■	■
Family Stage	Couple	Preschool	School-age	Adolescent

Figure 4. Critical Family Competencies, Supports, and Coping in Adaptation to Foreign and High-Risk Environments

DEVELOPMENTS IN FAMILY ADAPTATION:
CHANGING FAMILY PARADIGMS

The research just reviewed underscores several important developments in the way we view families and what predictions we dare make about the future of families in the United States. Certainly the current emphasis upon family strengths rather than family weaknesses is an important development. We have witnessed a growing emphasis upon programs designed to support families, to facilitate the development of family communication, sensitivity, awareness, understanding, and caring.[13] We see the emergence of programs designed to foster sexual awareness among partners and to promote communication between parent and child. Family life education has emerged with renewed interest and vitality as a tool for strengthening families.

The research would also indicate a greater awareness of and appreciation for the importance of family-to-community relationship transactions.[14] Families are not isolated from the social context in which they live; survival of the family unit depends upon the quality of this relationship and particularly upon social support. The family is called upon to give to and become involved in the community, and in return it expects to receive services, programs, and emotional as well as esteem support. In response to this need for a reciprocal exchange of resources between the family and the community, we have observed an increased emphasis upon self-help programs, social support groups, crisis centers, spiritual support groups, and church-community activities.

Family researchers have come to recognize and appreciate the very complex yet revealing relationship between family members and the total family unit and upon the family unit's relationship to the social community.[15] Out of this line of reasoning and enlightenment, we can begin to piece together the new rules and new images surrounding the family in a changing and stressful environment.

Social scientists have referred to the images we hold of

social situations as paradigms. Paradigms are ways of viewing. They change slowly and are important, because they influence how we respond to situations. For example, a 1960 image of Japanese products included such labels as cheap, copies, and poor quality. Today we have a new paradigm of Japanese industry which includes such kudos as quality, innovative, high tech, and excellence. Our way of viewing families is also important, and we need to be sensitive to what family paradigm shifts are occurring. One could argue that social scientists are in the midst of major changes in family paradigms, distinct and discernible shifts in the way we view families and the way families view their relationship to the world around them. These shifts may be apparent to the person on the street or in the pew. In the language of researchers, these emerging family paradigms are the following. We shall try to explain each of them below.

1. Psychosystems to Ecosystems
2. Anecdotal Descriptions to Scientific Assessment
3. Psychoengineering to Family-Community Engineering
4. Social Control to Empowering Families
5. Family Wellness to Family "Fitness"
6. Social Dependence to Self-Reliance and Sharing
7. Role Efficiency to Role Flexibility
8. Self-Fulfillment to Mutual Benefit
9. Treatment to Enrichment
10. Instrumental Support to Social Support

1. Psychosystems to Ecosystems. The family is viewed as an integral part of a nested set within the total ecosystem. All parts of the universe are related to each other and each component impacts upon the other. The family unit is one part of the total social and biological system. This is an important development in family research, for not only do we now focus upon the family's relationship to the world but, of equal importance, we are encouraged to examine how the family system influences the physical-cellular functioning of its members; family life has a bearing upon the biological functioning and well-being of its members.[16] Our traditional psychological view of the family is no longer sufficient for us to grasp fully the dynamics of family life.

2. Anecdotal Descriptions to Scientific Assessment. We are pressed to obtain more quantitative data on families and present such data as evidence supporting the value of families. We are no longer able to depend upon our emotional arguments, and the "family" expertise in each of us, to develop, shape, and seek support for programs and policies to support family life. High technology and the competition for limited space, dollars, and other resources have fostered a demand for "verifiable and documentable" evidence as to the merits of our arguments for and on behalf of families.[17] We have witnessed the emergence of a valued science in the study of the family, the increased sophistication and respectability of the field of family research, the advances in family assessment techniques in contrast to the clinical case descriptions, the demand for qualitative information supplemented by quantitative indices in support of observations and clinical hunches, and the use of family data in policy formulation and decision-making.

An example of this would be the Center on Corporate Responsibility's search for quantitative information to guide the development of their programs in support of families. (This Center is a Minneapolis group involving Minnesota Mining [3M], Honeywell, Control Data, and others.) Another example of the need for quantitative data relates to family practitioners who seek support for their argument that families play a critical role in prevention, treatment, and the rehabilitation of family members who are ill. The Native Hawaiian Education Assessment Project,[18] reported on earlier, may be offered as evidence of the demand for quantitative data to support our existing programs and services and to promote the need for new programs to serve the culturally disadvantaged.

3. Psychoengineering to Family-Community Engineering. We are witnessing greater efforts to shape the lives of families and the communities in which they live in a very systematic and purposeful way. Family policy considerations are now an integral and valued part of policy-making. Families shape the quality of the community and thus play an active part in the development of policies affecting them. An example of this would be the Army's effort to move total communities and family units from location to location, even from one part of the globe to another, as in the case of families moving to West Germany as a total group and the movement of families rotating back to Fort Hood, Texas.[19] Another example would be the increased emphasis upon home family monitoring in health care to facilitate communication between regional medical centers and families and to reduce the costs to families, as well as to improve the quality of care to whole family units. The increased emphasis upon using technology, such as microcomputers, to establish and maintain job banks (current) to facilitate the transition of families from one community to another on an international basis is still another example. While individual psychology is important, it is taking a backseat to the emerging interest in shaping the quality of family life through structuring the total community.

4. Social Control to Empowering Families. We are moving into an era in which greater efforts are made to empower families to be more independent and in control of the present and the future. We are witnessing the emergence of a social perspective and a societal interest in examining what more can be done to support families to be more self-sufficient—to do their job well. Efforts to empower families are reflected in the emergence of the National League of Families during and following the Vietnam War, and in the emergence of wives groups and family groups carrying on a dialogue with the U.S. Government with the intention of ensuring that their needs are met today and into the future.

Families are seeking to take control of their lives, insisting on making more decisions, questioning policies and programs that could undermine the family's stability, and insisting on information from policymakers that would help families to take charge of their destiny. Clearly, the family's efforts to demand quality medical care and medical information have empowered families in a positive way to be in charge of their health and well-being.

5. Family Wellness to Family "Fitness." We are placing a greater emphasis upon how and to what degree families "fit into the community in which they live" as a valid index of family adaptation.[20] Family functioning is being redefined to include the degree to which families are able to adapt to the social context in which they live. There is increased interest in the study of remarriages and serial marriages and how families negotiate and work out a satisfactory set of rules and processes designed to ensure a satisfactory fit among family members, between family units, and among family members from different family units. In other words, we are interested in understanding how families balance and fit the puzzle of meeting individual needs, family needs, and community needs. It is not sufficient to look at what can be done to strengthen the internal relationships of the family (e.g., enrichment programs, communication programs); one must also take into account family transactions, family negotiations, and community relationships.

6. Social Dependence to Self-Reliance and Sharing. Families are being called upon to take on added social responsibility, to care for the elderly, the mentally ill, and the handicapped. As more and more social programs fall by the wayside in the face of financial cuts at both the state and the federal level, families are called upon to shoulder the burdens.[21] But this self-reliance is complemented by an emerging value to "share" and to be "altruistic" in the process of coping with this change. Families are working together, sharing resources, and being mutually supportive in an effort to help families less able to cope with the situation. Certainly, we have witnessed a revival of patterns of mutual support within neighborhoods, among friends, and among relatives. This shift is in sharp contrast to our accustomed dependence on government to fill the gap and provide for families.

7. Role Efficiency to Role Flexibility. In this era of rapid social change, we have witnessed the emergence of a commitment to work toward greater role flexibility in both men and women, as part of the family's efforts to achieve the highest level of adaptation. At the same time, we are observing a movement away from traditional role structures in the family and toward an emphasis upon job sharing, task allocations, dual careers, dual wage earners, joint parenting, joint custody—all indices of a demand for greater role flexibility. This trend may be at the expense of the efficiency that characterized traditional role structures based on gender role allocations; everyone "knew" who did what.

8. Self-Fulfillment to Mutual Benefit. We have observed the emergence of a renewed interest in what will "benefit" all involved rather than what is "best" for one's self-fulfillment. In the face of alternative family structures, dual careers, dual wage earners, remarriages, multiple remarriages, and single-parenting, to name a few, family units and members involved are called upon to compromise, to seek "mutually beneficial" solutions in order for families to achieve a satisfactory level of adaptation. An increasing number of men are changing careers to accommodate the needs of the family unit and particularly the changing role of wives who are seeking to establish or reestablish careers and struggling to acquire skills needed to fulfill new roles inside and outside the family unit. Corporations are making an effort to develop job descriptions and corporate benefits (e.g., flexible benefits, day care) that will not only support families but benefit the corporation and its goals.

9. Treatment to Enrichment. There has been an increase in the number of family-oriented programs designed to enrich family life. This shift in emphasis emerges out of the philosophy that society can do more to help families to be strong and to endure in the face of rapid social change.[22] We have observed the development of family life centers in all branches of the Armed Forces, a proliferation of marital enrichment programs designed to support families throughout the life cycle, and the development of programs designed to facilitate family transitions through major changes such as the transition to parenthood or through hardship such as loss of employment.

10. Instrumental Support to Social Support. Families appear to benefit from the social contacts they develop within programs, and in direct contact with people, church affiliations, and friendships within the community. This type of support through natural groups and human contacts has healing quality in protecting families from adversity and in facilitating their adaptation following a major crisis. Families appear to benefit from emotional support, esteem support, network support, appraisal support, and altruistic support.[23] In other words, families are placing a greater emphasis upon social and human contacts to get the basic nurturance and understanding that are essential in managing stressful life events.

Ultimately, these shifts in paradigms affect the way we relate to and view families in this era of change, and are likely to have a profound impact upon family relationships over the life cycle. While René Dubos may be skeptical about the long-range consequences of family adaptation (we really cannot forecast the long-range outcomes, and fared so poorly, for example, in anticipating the problems of Hawaiian families), we have every reason to believe that the overall trend toward balancing family self-reliance and community support with personal strengths, including spiritual development, is likely to have a positive outcome. Families will not only endure but will thrive in this era of changing

roles and changing structures. What is our role as helpers?
Consider these observations:

- When families ask us to listen to them and we start giving
  them advice, we have not done what they asked.
- When they ask us to listen to them and we begin to tell
  them why they shouldn't be that way, we are trampling on
  their dignity and esteem.
- When they ask us to listen and we feel we have to do
  something to solve their problem, we have failed them,
  strange as that may seem.
- Listen! All they asked was that we listen, not talk or do,
  just hear them.
- Advice is cheap! A little change will get you Dear Abby and
  Billy Graham, in the same newspaper. But families can do
  for themselves; families are not helpless—discouraged and
  faltering, perhaps, but not helpless. When we do something for them that they can and need to do for themselves,
  we contribute to their weakness and fragileness.
- Perhaps that's why prayer works for some families. God
  doesn't give advice or fix things. God is just there, and
  listens, and lets us work it out for ourselves.
- So listen, and hear what families are saying. And if we
  wait our turn, they'll listen to us.

4

The Social Mission of the Family

James McGinnis and Kathleen McGinnis

"It's hard enough just trying to be a family at home. All this social action stuff seems like just too much for us right now."

"We're pretty heavily involved in a lot of this—the 'Freeze,' CROP walks, Central America—but I'm not sure we're doing a good job at home."

"I'm a single parent trying to support my family and have time for my own needs. How do you expect me to fit in the rest of the world?"

These comments are typical of many beleaguered parents trying to realize what it means to be "family." As a family, we have felt this tension ourselves, especially as the children are getting older and their problems more complex. When they say, "When I try to talk to you, it seems like you're always thinking about something else" or "Why can't you come to my play next week?" we wonder whether we are shortchanging our children, at least at times, for our involvement in social concerns. What all of us are seeking is the sense of wholeness or harmony that is expressed by the Hebrew word *shalom*. This wholeness is also connoted in the term "family." We want the intimacy, trust, concern, security, and togetherness of shalom/family not only for our homes but also for our neighborhoods and our world. But

most families do not see how they can do all three. And many
other families feel threatened by the larger world and by all
the changes they see around them. They see "family values"
under attack in the violence, sexual permissiveness, and
escalating rate of divorce in our society. Many also feel that
family is being threatened by all the fuss about the roles of
men and women in the home, society, and church and by
what they see as the politicization or secularization of their
church as it becomes more involved in social issues. They
long for a return to "family values."

What are these values? Dolores Curran's list of fifteen
traits of a healthy family closely resembles our own listing.[1]
"Togetherness" encompasses many of these values or traits
—communication and listening; sharing; time together, especially around meals; play; family rituals and celebrations.
Closely related is a second set that includes affection, affirmation, and support for each other. These values both imply
and reinforce a deep respect of the family members for each
other and for each person's individuality and need for pri-
vacy to complement the togetherness set of values. A third
set might include a sense of responsibility, mutual trust, and
a sense of right and wrong. Embodied in these general values
is a call both to a deep sense of fidelity—fidelity between
parent and child and, in marriage, fidelity between spouses
("in season and out of season," as Paul puts it)—and to a
concern for others, especially relatives and neighbors. Finally, "family values" includes a religious core—a concern
for prayer, for God.

While many families seem to feel that these values can
be realized only in the security of retreating from the
world, the thesis of this chapter is that family values are
realized not only by "spending more time with the family"
but also by participating as a family and with other families in the transformation of the world. To realize shalom
in the home itself means addressing shalom at all levels of
community—the home, the neighborhood, and the global
community. Family community is built in part by partici-

pation in the building of neighborhood and global community.

More and more of our churches are seeing the educational task of parents as an outward-looking one:

> Their [parents'] role as educators is so decisive that scarcely anything can compensate for their failure in it. For it devolves on parents to create a family atmosphere so animated with love and reverence for God and [people] that a well-rounded personal and social development will be fostered among the children. Hence, the family is the first school of those social virtues which every society needs.
>
> ... It is through the family that they are gradually introduced into civic partnership with their fellow [human beings], and into the People of God. Let parents, then, clearly recognize how vital a truly Christian family is for the life and development of God's own people.[2]

What this "civic partnership" and the "development of God's own people" are ultimately about is the transformation of the world and building the kingdom of God.

How Society Affects the Family

Before we consider how the Christian family can participate in the transformation of society, it is necessary to examine in some detail the various ways in which the larger society affects family life and values. Modern society is proving to be both blessing and curse for families trying to live and share the gospel message. Urbanization and other characteristics of modern society have created a whole set of new social problems. This section will examine five such problems. These are not the only ones affecting Christian families today. They are, however, problems that impact families in a special way and problems that families have a special role in challenging. These five problems affect people in all societies and cultures to varying degrees, but they are particularly prevalent in the affluent West.

Materialism

While modern capitalist and socialist economies have provided a more decent life in material terms for hundreds of millions of people, they have also created a very real problem for Christian families, and in capitalist societies the problem takes a special form. Pope Paul VI described it in specific terms:

> While very large areas of the population are unable to satisfy their primary needs, superfluous needs are ingeniously created. It can thus rightly be asked if, in spite of all [our] conquests, [we are] not turning back against [ourselves] the results of [our] activity. Having rationally endeavored to control nature, [are we] not now becoming the slave[s] of the objects which [we make]?[3]

"Slaves of the objects we make" describes the tendency in affluent societies for objects to become more important than persons. Objects are personified and persons are commodified. Even a cursory study of advertising reveals that objects provide us what persons are supposed to provide—identity, companionship, joy, intimacy. Persons are often treated as objects—sex objects, sales targets, units of labor. The effects of materialism—this commodification of the person—are particularly devastating on families.

More is better; happiness is having. Having things, having youth, having beauty becomes an all-consuming drive. Novelty becomes central—always getting something new. This drive takes a terrible toll on adults and children alike. The spiritual dimension of life is undermined, if not altogether lost. We seek recognition and affirmation in what we have rather than in who we are. Amassing swamps sharing. The more we seek security in money, goods, and huge insurance policies, the less we find our security in God and in each other. We are afraid to take risks for the gospel, for fear of their economic consequences. Fidelity to our spouse, our children, and our work becomes threatened as novelty is constantly dangled before us. This continual tantalizing of children as well as adults, of poor as well as rich, to get more things and to enjoy "the good life" threatens our very souls.

No wonder the Roman Catholic bishops of Appalachia wrote in their pastoral letter, *This Land Is Home to Me:*

> Many times before outside forces have attacked the mountain's dream. But never before was the attack so strong. Now it comes with cable TV, satellite communications, giant ribbons of highway driving into the guts of the land. The attack wants to teach people that happiness is what you buy—in soaps and drinks, in gimmicks and gadgets, and that all of life is one big commodity market. It would be bad enough if the attack only tried to take the land, but it wants the soul, too.[4]

Writing off the have-nots. If happiness is having things, youth, and beauty, what happens to those who do not have these? These "have-nots"—the economically poor, the elderly, the disabled, the not-so-beautiful people of our societies—are disregarded, disdained, discarded, and in some cases even destroyed.

Abusing the earth. The command of Genesis to subdue the earth calls us to be stewards of God's creation, to use the earth wisely, not to abuse its resources. But the prevailing "more is better" attitude is threatening the earth itself. We are all tempted by an attitude that says, "Who cares about future generations as long as I get mine."

A contrasting attitude, reverence for the earth as God's creation, leads to a reverence for persons, for future generations, and especially to reverence for the Creator. North American Indian parents have shared this value with their children for centuries, but it is an "endangered species" for many others in our materialistic world. This concern was prophetically addressed by a group of Canadian church leaders:

> In the final analysis what is required is nothing less than fundamental social change. Until we as a society begin to change our own life styles based on wealth and comfort, until we begin to change the profit-oriented priorities of our industrial system, we will continue placing exorbitant demands on the limited supplies of energy in the North and end up exploiting the people of the North in order to get those resources. . . .

Ultimately, the challenge before us is a test of our faithfulness in the living God. For we believe that the struggle for justice and responsible stewardship in the North today, like that in distant Third World countries, is the voice of the Lord among us. We are called to involve ourselves in these struggles, to become active at the very center of human history where the great voice of God cries out for the fullness of life.[5]

How families can respond to this appeal will be explored below.

Individualism

Closely related to materialism is the kind of individualism that is especially fostered in capitalist societies. This is not the individualism that pushes each person to do his or her best to see that personal needs are fulfilled, and to value personal freedoms. Rather, it is a consistent lifting up of self over all other considerations. One manifestation of this problem is a mentality that exalts possessions. A second manifestation is the separation of personal freedom from its social context. One Christian church's expression of this concern claims that we cannot adhere to a capitalism that

exalts individual freedom by withdrawing it from every limitation, by stimulating it through exclusive seeking of interest and power, and by considering social solidarities as more or less automatic consequences of individual initiatives, not as an aim and a major criterion of the value of the social organization.[6]

This lack of concern for the common good is partially a consequence of a third manifestation of individualism—the private property ethic as understood and practiced in our capitalist society. Private ownership entitles me to use my resources any way I want, says the culture. Not so, say Christian churches. For example:

The recent Council [Vatican II] reminded us of this: "God intended the earth and all that it contains for the use of every human being and people. Thus, as all [persons] follow justice and unite in charity, created goods should abound for them on a reasonable basis." All other rights whatsoever, including those of property and of free commerce, are to subordinated to this principle. . . .

In a word, "according to the traditional doctrine as found in the Fathers of the Church and the great theologians, the right to property must never be exercised to the detriment of the common good."[7]

In a similar vein, a Presbyterian (U.S.A.) study document declares:

The doctrine of creation affirms that material things are given for *all* humankind to enjoy.

. . . God's good creation is not given just for the privileged few. It is for all people to share and enjoy. All are to have fair access. And future generations are to have their fair share as well.[8]

This kind of individualism weighs heavily on families. The highly competitive nature of our economic system and society, combined with the image of "rugged individuals raising themselves up by their own bootstraps," plus high mobility and an increase in nuclear and one-parent households, has isolated many families. This isolation has increased the need for material security, with the consequences thereof pointed out earlier. Children and adults alike see others as competitors—for grades, for jobs, for affection, for position, prestige, and power. Genuine Christian community becomes much more difficult. Supportive, noncompetitive relationships, even within families, become more difficult as competitive relationships permeate the society as a whole. The more that family members pursue personal goals to the detriment of the common good of family and society, the more it is that fractured and unhappy families seem to increase.

In public policy issues, materialism and individualism contribute to devastating situations. Governments and economic systems that permit inadequate wages, tolerate double-digit inflation, and allow high unemployment—in short, that do not guarantee the basic necessities of life to each person and family—place great burdens on families. Often both parents are forced to work long hours. Sometimes

unemployed fathers are forced to leave their home if the
other family members are to receive even minimal assistance. Unemployment—whether the cause is automation,
multinational corporations closing factories for cheaper
labor elsewhere, government budget cuts, or failure to plan
and direct more capital to more job-creating industries—has
its spiritual or psychological effects as well as physical and
economic effects on workers and their families:

> As lamentable as these financial costs are, the social and
> human impact is far more deplorable. In our society, persons
> without a job lose a key measure of their place in society and a
> source of individual fulfillment; they often feel that there is no
> productive role for them. Many minority youth may grow up
> without meaningful job experiences and come to accept a life of
> dependency. Unemployment frequently leads to higher rates of
> crime, drug addiction, and alcoholism. It is reflected in higher
> rates of mental illness as well as rising social tensions. The idle-
> ness, fear and financial insecurity resulting from unemploy-
> ment can undermine confidence, erode family relationships,
> dull the spirit and destroy dreams and hopes. One can hardly
> bear to contemplate the disappointment of a family which has
> made the slow and painful climb up the economic ladder and
> has been pushed down once again into poverty and dependence
> by the loss of a job.[9]

Racism

The connection between the problems that families face in
our society because of our economic system and the problem
of racism is clearly pointed out in the U.S. Roman Catholic
Bishops' pastoral letter on racism, *Brothers and Sisters to
Us:*

> Racism and economic oppression are distinct but interrelated
> forces which dehumanize our society. Movement toward authen-
> tic justice demands a simultaneous attack on both evils. Our
> economic structures are undergoing fundamental changes which
> threaten to intensify social inequalities in our nation. We are

> entering an era characterized by limited resources, restricted job
> markets and dwindling revenues. In this atmosphere, the poor
> and racial minorities are being asked to bear the heaviest burden
> of the new economic pressures. . . . As economic pressures
> tighten, those people who are often black, Hispanic, Native
> American and Asian—and always poor—slip further into the
> unending cycle of poverty, deprivation, ignorance, disease, and
> crime. . . . The economic pressures exacerbate racism, particu-
> larly where poor white people are competing with minorities for
> limited job opportunities.[10]

The connection between materialism and individualism on
the one hand and racism on the other is also noted in this
pastoral letter. "Today's racism flourishes in the triumph of
private concern over public responsibility, individual success over social commitment, and personal fulfillment over
authentic compassion."[11]

In terms of some specific facts of racism and their effects
on families, unemployment among various minority groups
in the United States is double (for Hispanic), triple (for
black), and eight times (for Native Americans on reserva-
tions) that of white Americans. For minority youth, it is even
worse.

Second, stereotypes of minority people continue to infect
television, toys, movies, books, even school textbooks. The
lack of positive self-images of minority people in these areas
affects both children and adults in minority groups. Low
self-esteem for many minority children and a superiority
complex for many white children is one result.

Third, racism in education is manifested in lower teacher
expectation for minority students; the lack of positive role
models, either as staff members or resource people; the lack
of decision-making power for minority people; situations
where minority students predominate in remedial classes
and whites in accelerated classes. Put very simply, racism in
education means that minority students are shortchanged.
They do not get the kind of education they need to prepare
them psychologically and academically for adult life.

Last, the growing housing crisis that plagues minority families, coupled with the low self-esteem of many unemployed fathers in minority groups and the glaring lack of supportive service to minority families, has a devastating effect on these families.

Sexism

Similar to racism in its dynamic is discrimination based on sex. The economic consequences of sexism are becoming more evident as more and more women join the work force because of economic need. Unequal pay for the same jobs and unequal access to more responsible and higher paying jobs often create serious problems for families where it is a woman's income that supports the family. For minority women there is a double burden of discrimination.

The cultural consequences of sexism are perhaps less blatant but no less serious for families and thus for the society as a whole. Stereotypes of what it means to be a "man" and what it means to be a "woman" limit the emotional, physical, and spiritual development of men and women, boys and girls. For instance, nurturing and serving continue to be seen in most families as the woman's role. Often the result is females locked into service roles and males restricted in the development of the nurturing, service dimension of the whole person. As with racial stereotypes, sex-role stereotypes infect the books children and adults read, the toys children play with, and the ads, television shows, and movies we all see.

Another stereotype that has a profound effect on family life relates to what was said above about materialism. Friendships between men and women and marital fidelity are threatened as women (and sometimes men, too) are seen more and more as sex objects. This finds blatant expression in pornography and more subtle but pervasive expression in advertising, television, and movies. For example, women are told in many ways that it is their appearance that will get and hold their mate and bring them happiness.

Violence and Militarism

Violence as a means of resolving conflicts, from interpersonal to international conflicts, does not seem to be decreasing. Military budgets in country after country continue to increase. The pursuit of security through bigger and better locks, police forces, prisons, armies, and nuclear warheads is growing.

This growing violence and militarism has a number of frightening consequences, for families and for society as a whole. Militarism as part of the national mentality manifests itself when schoolchildren in Michigan are recruited in a contest to design an insignia for a new Trident submarine, a "first strike" weapon with 408 nuclear warheads, each with destructive capacity of 2,040 Hiroshimas. A seven-year-old boy in Missouri is rewarded with a $20 bill for "drawing blood" (knocking a tooth out) from an opponent in a league football game. Spouse abuse and child abuse are especially frightening manifestations of the escalating violence in our society today.

Militarism affects families on the economic level as well. Some $300 billion in U.S. military expenditures for the fiscal year is a major reason why families cannot find adequate food, shelter, medical care, and education. "Demonic" and "an unparalleled waste of human and material resources" in the view of the World Council of Churches,[12] the arms race has also been described by the Vatican as "an act of aggression which amounts to a crime, for even when they are not used, by their costs alone armaments kill the poor by causing them to starve."[13]

FAMILY PARTICIPATION IN THE
CHURCH'S SOCIAL MISSION

The Social Mission of the Church

To preach the gospel demands that we address these social problems. From a Roman Catholic perspective, "action on behalf of justice and participation in the transformation of the world fully appear to us as a constitutive dimension of the preaching of the Gospel, or, in other words, of the Church's mission for the redemption of the human race and its liberation from every oppressive situation."[14] That part of the church's social mission is to confront the oppressive situations and structures described above is equally a Presbyterian Church priority is clear from the peacemaking priority adopted by the 192d General Assembly (1980):

> The Reformed tradition of Christian faith has been historically committed to world-transforming action. Reconciliation to God has included reconciliation to the neighbor and action in the social, political, and economic realms for the sake of just order and peace.[15]

This commitment is reflected in the Presbyterian approach to educational ministry as well:

> Knowing that God is creating the New Humanity, the church's vocation is to exhibit a new quality of life; serve others in the world; exercise responsibility in the household, on the job, in community organizations, and work for the transformation of cultural, political and economic institutions—consistent with the vision and values of God's commonwealth.[16]

In other words, it is not sufficient to care for the victims of injustice—the corporal works of mercy. It is also necessary to work to change the situations and structures (economic, political, cultural) that create the victims in the first place —the works of justice.

"Family responsibilities" do not exclude families from participating in this world-transforming task. In fact, Christian churches are explicitly challenging families to participate:

> The family must also see to it that the virtues of which it is the teacher and guardian should be enshrined in laws and institutions. It is of the highest importance that families should together devote themselves directly and by common agreement to transforming the very structure of society. Otherwise, families will become the first victims of the evils that they will have watched idly and with indifference.[17]

It belongs to the laity, without waiting passively for orders and directives, to take the initiative freely and to infuse a Christian spirit into the mentality, customs, laws and structures of the community in which they live.[18]

How Christian families specifically can be part of this mission will be elaborated upon shortly. First, though, it is important to look at some of the obstacles preventing families from participation and at a general strategy for overcoming these obstacles.

Obstacles Limiting Family Participation

The social context of family life presents a number of obstacles to families participating in the church's social mission. Among these obstacles are the five social problems identified earlier in the chapter. Other obstacles include a lack of inspiration, lack of imagination, and lack of integration of the various aspects of Christian living.

Faced with so many problems of their own, many families are not inspired to work with and for others. Economic insecurity and other fears keep them from the risks involved in social action. Often isolated from the victims of injustice, from people working for change, and from a supportive community, many families have just not been touched or moved to want to act.

Sometimes families are inspired to act, but do not know what to do. Lack of imagination and insight often keeps them from acting, especially when the social problems seem so complex and overwhelming. The more out of touch we are with the victims of injustice and with people working for change, the less imaginative as well as less courageous we are likely to be.

Lack of integration closely relates to this lack of imagination. Time is one dimension of this obstacle. Active Christian parents are among the most beleaguered of people—raising children, nurturing a marriage relationship or other supportive relationships in a home, being involved in school and church, trying to survive financially, actively participating in their neighborhood. Poor families and single-parent families generally have even less time and more sources of frustration. Unless parents can begin to see how to bring family life and social action together, they will never have time for both.

But more and more families are beginning to discover how their working in the world as a family community is enriching that family community. Generally, in this regard, parents are growing and learning right along with their children. Together, they are sharing their feelings about acting for justice. The time spent as a family to explain, choose, plan, and pray over family social actions fosters family community. Sometimes a parent and a child discover new dimensions of each other as persons and appreciate each other more in the process. The family deepens its sense of identity, significance, and pride by participating together in the church's social mission. And it is amazing how much of this mission can be expressed within the context of parenting.

Not that it always works out so neatly or that every family takes social mission so seriously all the time. For instance, on the ride back to Boston College from a visit to the Kennedy Library one summer, we were telling our children how important the witness of Robert Kennedy had been in shaping our own commitment and how inspirational the morning tour had been for us. Recalling how engaged they seemed to be in the tour as well, we asked the children what the highlight of the visit was for each of them. After some silence, David, age eleven, asked, "Does the lettuce and tomato on my sandwich count for my vegetable for lunch today?"

The other dimension of the lack of integration, besides time, is the dichotomy many people still experience between their personal spirituality and social action. Some Christians, parents included, do not participate in the church's social mission, because they do not see such participation as an essential expression of their faith. They do not recognize the call to transform the world as a call from Jesus. Instead, they often regard it as something for social activists and "secular humanists."

Some Components in a Strategy
for Overcoming These Obstacles

The inspiration, imagination, and integration needed for the church's social mission to take root in one's heart will call for a conversion for many Christians. Among the components in this conversion process are the following three:

1. Experiencing social ministry as a call from Jesus. The more that the call to social ministry is seen as a call from Jesus, the more likely a person is to respond. Fostering a personal relationship with Jesus, especially through prayer and thoughtful reflection on the Scriptures, is essential. Parents doing this with their children, religious educators with their students, and ministers with parents and children can lead families to hear the voice of God:

> Is not this the sort of fast that pleases me
> —it is the Lord Yahweh who speaks—
> to break unjust fetters
> and undo the thongs of the yoke,
> to let the oppressed go free,
> and break every yoke,
> to share your bread with the hungry,
> and shelter the homeless?
> (Isa. 58:6–7, JB)

Blessed are those who hunger and thirst for righteousness. . . . Blessed are the peacemakers. (Matt. 5:6, 9)

If we know more and more the Jesus who says this to us, walks with us as we follow his call, then we will be more willing to say yes.

The liturgical year retells the life of Jesus and thus his social mission. To make this mission explicit in the celebration of the liturgical year is essential in the conversion process. Advent and Christmas speak to us of God taking the

world so seriously as to become human, of the coming of
Jesus in simplicity to serve and not be served, of Jesus as the
Prince of Peace. Lent marks the call to repentance for social
sin as well as personal sin, the call to respond to Jesus as his
passion is relived in the suffering of the hungry, the victims
of racism and repression, the elderly, and so forth. Easter
and Pentecost are the source of our hope and courage.

The Lord's Supper itself calls us to build the unity of the
body of Christ which we symbolize and celebrate in that
Sacrament:

> The Lord's Supper, together with baptism, expresses the charter,
> covenant-establishing event of Jesus' death-resurrection, by
> which we are incorporated into the covenant community. The
> Lord's Supper is God serving us, and it is our thankful response.
> In our responsive sacrifice, Calvin said, "are included all the
> duties of love." Radical self-giving should be the outcome. . . .
> Receiving the Lord's Supper and living out the social implica-
> tions of the Supper are one. Body broken "for the life of the
> world" (John 6:51) and blood "poured out for many" (Mark 14:24)
> carry cosmic, world-wide implications. . . . Life itself must become
> the dynamic prolongation of the Lord's Supper.[19]

2. Being touched by the victims and by advocates for justice. As noted above, the victims of injustice as well as others
working hard for justice can touch our hearts and move us
to action. Their struggles and witness can help us overcome
our complacency and fears.

3. Being supported in community. The support of others
also helps us overcome our fears. Working with other families increases the effectiveness of our social action. Working
with others provides both accountability and challenge. The
example of others challenges us to live more faithfully. It is
easier to run away, as it were, when no one else is around.
Finally, working with other families often provides the necessary ingredient of enjoyment. Children especially need to
enjoy social involvement if they are to integrate it into their
own lives. Having other children along makes a real difference in many cases. And having other adults along also

makes a real difference to parents, especially those who are parenting by themselves.

This was brought home to us several years ago when our oldest son, nine at the time, was adamant about not wanting to join us in serving a meal at a local soup kitchen and family shelter. He explained that his first experience there was difficult because some of the older children at the shelter were a lot tougher than he was. It was not until we stumbled onto the idea of having him invite a friend to go along that he was willing to return with us. Families that come together regularly to pray, play, or share in other ways sometimes evolve into groups that share economic resources and involve themselves more fully in the church's social mission. It is in such communities of families and other individuals that much of the hope for the church's social mission resides.

SPECIFIC WAYS FOR FAMILIES TO PARTICIPATE IN THE CHURCH'S SOCIAL MISSION

The suggestions that follow relate specifically to the five social problems identified earlier and are organized into three categories. First, there are life-style changes, those ways in which families can begin to live in ways and according to values different from those embodied in the culture. Second, there are the works of mercy by which families can respond to the immediate needs of people who are the victims of the materialism, individualism, racism, sexism, and violence in our society. Third, there are the works of justice, ways in which families can challenge the institutions or structures of society that embody anti-Christian values or whose policies cause or contribute to injustice. Part of this challenging of institutions is the creation of alternative institutions.

Materialism and Individualism

Living the alternative. Fidelity to another person, whether it is parent to child or married partners to one another, is a powerful sign in our age. This fidelity witnesses to commitment over novelty, to love and community over exploitation and individualism. Family can also be a living school of simplicity and stewardship. Involving the children in the family's recycling efforts is a basic way for all to care for the earth's resources. Economic s ɩring—whether it is families sharing tools or outgrown clothes or whether it is a community of families in which incomes are pooled and divided according to need—witnesses to the vision of gospel security and community spelled out in The Acts of the Apostles. Stewardship and simplicity of heart also flow out of deep reverence for the earth. Family or community gardens, hiking, camping trips, a walk through the park with a child (when our own children were younger, such moments were few and far between) can all put us in touch with creation and the Creator. They provide opportunities to experience beauty and to learn to care for it.

Sharing our goods with the poor. For most families, their home is their most precious possession. Treating our home, as well as our other possessions, as a gift from God that is meant for service or sharing with the wider community is a significant way of making stewardship concrete for families. Opening our home to a person needing temporary or longer-term shelter—a teenager who cannot make it at home, an overnight traveler, an elderly relative, a foster child—is welcoming the Lord. If a family is able, emotionally as well as financially, to take someone else in, such a sharing of the home can have a deep impact on the children. They clearly participate daily in such an action.

Challenging institutions that encourage materialism and individualism. Because one crucial source of materialism and selfish individualism is advertising, an important task for parents and teachers is to help children become conscious and critical of how they are manipulated by advertising, packaging, and the other ways they are being urged to buy things. Television advertising is especially troublesome. Watching commercials with children and pointing out or asking them to point out some of the techniques being used is a first step for parents. Further, corporate sponsors and the media need to hear the prophetic voice of Christian families. Family letters are one possibility. Families have participated in consumer boycotts of corporations pursuing maximization of profit at the expense of people. Sometimes, though, parents need to check out whether their children really understand what the issue is. We overheard our son Tom, age ten at the time, explaining to a friend why our family was participating in the boycott of Nestlé products: "They [Nestlé] put infant formula in their candy bars and that makes poor babies sick."

Supporting alternative institutions that do not exploit people or the earth is another approach. Thus, many families buy their fruits and vegetables directly from small farmers or are part of a local food cooperative, as an alternative to the growing control over North American food production by giant agribusiness corporations. Church or neighborhood credit unions offer families and others an alternative to commercial banks that sometimes write off poorer neighborhoods.

Racism

Living the alternative. The development of healthy racial attitudes in children and assisting children to experience and desire a more multicultural and multiracial world are an important dimension of the family's social mission. Because the home environment is so crucial in the formation of racial attitudes, families should focus there first. Do the visuals—so important in early learning—in the home (pictures, magazines, toys, books) portray a variety of peoples and cultures?

As we look at the wider environment, we see important experiences that shape racial attitude. Are neighborhood, school, church, and shopping center multicultural or monocultural environments? If the people who provide important services for the family, such as teachers and physicians, are all white, then children are learning that only white people do important things. If the wider environment is monocultural, it is more difficult to provide children and adults with those experiences—contacts, friendships—that promote respect and appreciation for people of all races and cultures.

Challenging institutions perpetuating racial stereotypes. Institutions help shape attitudes. Thus, we need to do more than provide multicultural books and toys for our children to offset those which portray only white characters or portray minority characters in stereotypic ways. Parents need to provide more racially accurate toys and to remove toys that are racially offensive. Teachers, curriculum developers, and textbook publishers can all be encouraged to find or develop multicultural materials.

Sexism

Living the alternative. At the level of the individual family, there are as many ways of dealing with sex-role stereotypes as there are with racial stereotyping. In families where there are both male and female role models, more equitable sharing of household tasks could be encouraged. In single-parent homes, by necessity, this kind of non-stereotyped modeling often is the practice. All parents can be careful about the kinds of messages they give children about what are "appropriate" tasks for men and women. Similarly, parents can and should promote a diversity of physical, intellectual, and artistic capabilities in their children. Many societies continue to limit such diversity, for both girls and boys, but especially for girls. Parents also need to concern themselves with internal qualities in their children. That is, caring, nurturing, and sensitive qualities are as important for boys as for girls. Assertive, independent, decisive, inventive qualities are as important for girls as for boys.

Challenging institutions perpetuating sex-role stereotypes. Unfortunately, sexism as well as racism permeate many of our schools. Parents can challenge sexism in the curriculum by urging schools to examine their instructional materials and to supplement the materials that fail adequately to present nonsexist images and the contributions of women to the world. As with racial stereotyping, toys, books, and the media are an important focus of family action. Sexism in our churches also needs to be challenged. Children as well as adults can work for greater participation for women of all ages in church functions and leadership positions.

Violence and Militarism

Living the alternative. The development of nonviolent and cooperative attitudes and skills in children is an important responsibility of parents and a way by which families can help create alternative attitudes and models in regard to the prevailing violence in our society. This responsibility can be exercised in a variety of ways. First, parents can create an affirming, cooperative, accepting environment in which nonviolent attitudes and skills are nurtured. Affirmation also encourages social involvement. No adult or child gets involved in social action for very long without a sense of self-worth or self-confidence. When risks are involved—even such things as "What will the other kids think?"—it is the people who feel good about themselves who can stand up for their beliefs.

A cooperative environment is also essential, as violence is nurtured by excessive competition. Family chores can be structured in such a way that they will involve persons working together. Cooperative games can balance competitive games. But even with our emphasis on fun in sports rather than just winning, our ten-year-old daughter was hesitant to enter a community "fun run" unless there was a trophy at the end. Family prayer contributes as well, especially when leadership is shared among all family members. Stewardship of our talents—sharing them with family members and others—promotes this cooperative spirit and environment.

An accepting, forgiving environment does much to reduce tension, diffuse resentment, and thereby promote nonviolent ways of dealing with conflict. One necessary ingredient for such an environment is for parents to feel good about themselves and their relationships. For couples the essential harmony of marital love is both nurtured by and nurturing of acceptance and forgiveness within the family.

In all these ways, families create that love described by Paul in the letter to the Ephesians:

> If we live by the truth and in love, we shall grow in all ways into Christ, who is the head by whom the whole body is fitted and joined together, every joint adding its own strength, for each separate part to work according to its function. So the body grows until it has built itself up, in love. (Eph. 4:15–16, JB)

> Be subject to one another out of reverence for Christ. (Eph. 5:21)

Where there is an environment of affirmation, cooperation, and acceptance, parents can convey to their children the attitudes, values, and skills of nonviolence. The skills include basic communication and conflict resolution skills that can generate alternative solutions in conflict situations. The promotion of regular family meetings or councils is one way of structuring such nonviolent conflict resolution into family life. Developing alternatives to violent (psychological as well as physical) forms of discipline is also crucial. The more violence is used on children, the more violence will be used by children.

Challenging institutions that promote violence. As we pointed out with regard to materialism, the media is an important institution on which to focus family action. Violence on television—in cartoons as well as in many prime time shows—has a negative effect on children. Besides challenging the extent of such programming, parents can spend time with their children talking over the violence they do encounter on television. This is also true of actual violence in the world, whether experienced in the neighborhood or seen on the news.

There are at least two approaches that families can take to challenge the growing militarism in our society. The first is more indirect. Instead of the "us against them" attitudes on which militarism thrives, we can educate ourselves and our children to the global nature of God's family. Pairing with, as well as praying for, sisters and brothers in other parts of the world can put us personally in touch with this global reality. Individual families as well as congregations have paired with families and congregations in other countries. Here, again, the kinds of artifacts, magazines, and people that come into our homes help shape our attitudes and the breadth of our awareness.

In these and other ways, families can help promote a sense of patriotism that is consistent with the gospel and does not pit one people or nation against another. A Roman Catholic expression of such patriotism is paralleled by a statement of the 192d General Assembly of the United Presbyterian Church U.S.A. (1980):

> Citizens should develop a generous and loyal devotion to their country, but without any narrowing of mind. In other words, they must always look simultaneously to the welfare of the whole human family, which is tied together by the manifold bonds linking races, peoples, and nations.[20]

> We are Christ's people, compelled by the Spirit and guided by our creeds to listen to a gospel that is addressed to the whole world. We are gathered around the Lord's Table with people from North and South and East and West. A new integrity is required of us: integrity in worship, integrity in secular life, integrity in relationship with Christ and Christians everywhere. . . . As God's people, we will seek the security of the whole human family—all for whom Christ died. As God's people, we will celebrate the dignity of each of God's children.[21]

At the same time that parents foster a sense of global awareness in their children, they can also undertake more direct challenges of institutions fostering militarism. Family letters to political representatives on the need to reverse the arms race is one step. Tax resistance is still illegal and therefore risky and beyond most of us. Nevertheless, it can be seen to be implied in the church's teaching on noncooperation with evil. Families need help in facing this issue. Some parents have taken such steps, if only symbolically, and have involved their children in the process. Other families have participated in public demonstrations to give prophetic witness for gospel values and against specific expressions of what they consider to be an immoral militarism.

CONCLUSION: A RETURN TO FAMILY VALUES

While most families would not consider some of the above actions and activities as part of family life, more and more families are coming to see that the gospel of Jesus asks such radical stances from his followers. Those families who are beginning to see this and who are supported in their response by a Christian community are bearing witness to the rest of us to be more willing to risk for the gospel. It is clear from church teaching that families have a definite responsibility to address these pressing social problems that cause injustice, threaten human life and dignity, and undermine family life itself. In so doing, each family, as one among many families in the world, finds fulfillment in service to others.

But it is not only the "concern for others" aspect of the list of family values that is realized in this understanding of family participation in the church's social mission. All the other family values are realized as well:

• The "togetherness" set of values is furthered by all the suggestions above on living the alternative to violence, especially the communication and conflict resolution skills and the family meeting; by the simplicity/stewardship suggestions involving sharing of talents and alternative celebrations that focus on people rather than things; and by the family's developing a sense of common mission and one they experience with other families.

- The affirmation and mutual support values are promoted by the centrality of peacemaking in the home itself—again, all the suggestions on living the alternative to violence. Challenging sex-role stereotypes and racial stereotypes affirms and promotes the full human development of each family member. Working with other families, encouraging risk-taking, and supporting one another in actions of all kinds also promote these family values.

- Family members' sense of responsibility and sense of right and wrong are furthered by shared decision-making through the family and the implementation of such decisions. The stewardship suggestions on caring for the earth and for future generations as well as sharing talents with family members and others nurture a deep sense of responsibility. Discussing social problems, encouraging one another to form opinions and stand up for what each believes—all promote these family values.

- The family value of concern for God, the gospel, and prayer is central to the whole vision of family life articulated in this chapter. It is Jesus who calls family members to participate in actions that build up the whole body of Christ. It is the resurrection of Jesus that gives family members the hope that if they die to themselves in embracing one another for life and in embracing a suffering world, their seeds will bear much fruit. It is the spirit of Jesus—encountered in contemplation, action, and in coming together prayerfully with others—that inspires and gives family members the courage to take the risks necessary to build shalom/family/community—the family community, the neighborhood community, and the global community.

5

The Importance of the Family: A Reformed Theological Perspective

Sang H. Lee

The nature and function of the family is today both an urgent and a difficult question to discuss. For one thing, what the term "family" refers to is not easy to determine. As everyone knows, many people no longer live in traditional families—families with parents, grandparents, children, and so on. Many families are now headed by a single parent, usually without the presence of grandparents. But more important, the so-called nuclear family, experts tell us, lost many of the family's traditional functions. The productive, protective, educational, recreational, religious, and status-giving functions have, in varying degrees, been transferred to the state and other social and religious institutions. Only the "affectional" function (procreation, the nurturing of children, intimacy, enduring love and support, etc.) seems to remain for the family to fulfill.[1]

The assessment by social scientists of the present condition of the family is not unanimous. Some have interpreted the reduction of the family's functions as a serious "weakening" of the family as a social unit and have predicted the inevitable rise of various alternative life-styles. But there is

I am grateful to Profs. Charles West and Donald Capps for their helpful comments on the earlier version of this chapter and to Profs. Freda Gardner and Craig Dykstra for sharing with me their perspectives on the topic.

a significant and growing body of scholarly opinion in the more positive direction. The family seems to have, according to recent studies, a "staying power" in spite of the transference of some of its functions to other social agencies. It can also be suggested that the remaining affectional function of the family as the place of enduring love and fidelity may indeed be the most essential function that the family has always fulfilled.[2] Implicit in such a view is the possibility that now that families are "freed" from many of their traditional functions, they may be able to function more fully than ever before as a place of personal nurture and interaction. The necessity for such a place of enduring love and belonging is great indeed in today's world of high mobility and rootlessness.

Even if we take a positive view toward the family's potential in its affectional function, however, its actual fulfillment of this function may be another matter. Individualism, for example, is still deeply ingrained in American culture and may make the family solidarity difficult to maintain. The effects of individualism can also be seen within the family. The growing ethos toward personal happiness and freedom may make the family a haven of privatized security and comfort without any orientation toward the public world.[3] In short, the family is here to stay and still may be able to fulfill its most essential function, but it faces at the same time many external and internal threats and problems.

This presence of both possibilities and problems in today's family makes it all the more important and urgent that those who belong to the Christian community press toward a theological understanding of the family. What is the exact nature of the family's importance in the Christian perspective? What is our theological understanding of the problems of today's family? Can Christian faith transform today's families in such a way that they can truly fulfill their destiny? And if so, how? How is the human family related to the new reality of the redeemed community of Christ, "the family of God"? What is the church's responsibility in relation to the family? These are some of the questions the church must ask. What is offered in this essay is meant to be a small contribution to this theological work.

We will use as our working definition of the family "a kinship system of two or more persons which involves a commitment to one another over time," and kinship is achieved by marriage, birth, or adoption.[4] This definition is not meant to deny that there may be other groupings of persons in which genuine community exists. We choose to work with this definition in order to point to the family as an inevitable and basic structure or setting in which human beings are at least initially placed to start their lives. The term "family" is indeed used more broadly than that and often as a metaphor. But such broad uses would be meaningful only if we are clear about the more elemental or basic sense of it. With this working definition of the family, we can now proceed to a theological discussion of its meaning and destiny.

The task of a theologian is to interpret the never-ending interplay between the concrete situation of the present moment, on the one hand, and the revelation of God's will in Jesus Christ and the history of Israel as recorded in the Scriptures and as faithfully interpreted with the help of the Holy Spirit, on the other. There is a kind of priority of God's revelation in Jesus Christ and in the Scriptures, but this priority becomes a living and relevant priority only as we faithfully restate and reread God's prior revelation in the concrete context of the present. So we ask, What is God's will and purpose for the still very basic human institution called "the family"?

In a short essay such as this, we do not have the space to delineate all the details and steps involved in the theological interplay between the revelation and the present predicament. What we propose to do is to state, first of all, a list of theological presuppositions that represent at least one interpretation of God's revelation, and then see what they say about the particular situation of the human family today.

In Protestant theology, the family has often been discussed within the dialectic of the orders of creation and

redemption—that is, the way things basically are as God
created the world and the way God in Jesus Christ has begun
to transform all things from their fallen state. And the family in Protestant thought has sometimes been considered as
belonging to the order of creation and not to the order of
redemption. There is no problem with this strategy to the
extent that it acknowledges the necessity of all things to be
redeemed. However, the key issue about which we need to be
clear is exactly how the order of creation and the order of
redemption are related, and how much value is assigned to
the order of creation. If a sharp contrast is drawn between
the two orders without a due stress upon their distorted and
yet abiding continuity, the order of creation (including the
family) drops out of the realm of ultimate importance. Helmut Thielicke, a distinguished German theologian and ethi-
cist, for example, sees marriage and by implication family as
essentially a "worldly" institution which preserves humanity so that God's redemptive work can be played out.[5] In this
scheme, the order of creation tends to function as a backdrop
for God's main act of redemption in Christ. A 1968 document
of the former United Presbyterian Church, entitled "The
Church's Educational Ministry to Families," adopts basically the same approach. Families belong to the order of
creation and thus are not part of the locus of God's redemptive work. The same document does acknowledge that families can be important as "a means of bearing witness to God's
grace" but keeps them essentially out of the realm of redemption.[6]

Again, it needs to be emphasized that humanity is in a
radically fallen condition and needs to be transformed by
God's grace. There is a discontinuity between creation and
redemption, nature and grace. However, in the two cases
just mentioned, there is a tendency toward a dualism between the two orders, a dualism between God the Creator
and God the Redeemer. For the Reformed theological tradition, the discontinuity between nature and grace is important, but so is the basic continuity between them. God the

Redeemer is the same God who creates and re-creates. Redemption is a restoration of what was inherently and originally good as well as a new creation from the distorted condition of that originally good creation. A fully trinitarian theology in the Calvinist tradition would somehow have to maintain a strong emphasis upon the discontinuity between the order of creation as it exists in its fallen state and the order of redemption *and* also upon an abiding connectedness between the two orders.

The theological perspective I wish to use as our guide is the American tradition within Reformed theology, represented by Jonathan Edwards. His is a highly theocentric, trinitarian, and Christ-focused perspective in which God's creative and redemptive works are closely related and at the same time clearly distinguished from each other. Edwards' brand of Reformed theology puts a high premium on God's intentions for creation itself and sees God's end in creation as the sanctification of temporal existence here and now as well as the complete consummation of that "end" in the eternal life.[7]

THEOLOGICAL PRESUPPOSITIONS

1. *The end for which God created the world is God's glorification of God's own being—namely, the repetition in time and space of the supreme beauty of the self-giving love within God's inner-trinitarian life.* The most important theological question for Jonathan Edwards is, Why did God create the world? rather than, How can I find a gracious Redeemer? Human beings start their history by sinning—that is, moving away from their vocation to participate in God's own work of attaining the ultimate end in creation. Thus, God's creative activity vis-à-vis the world becomes a work of redemption. Redemption is the central content of God's providential activity. God is our gracious Redeemer. But Edwards puts the initial question in a God-centered, rather than human-centered, way. The fundamental focus is on God's own

goal of sanctifying God's entire creation so that every being in it becomes a finite and yet real repetition of God's internal beauty.

Everything in the realm of creation is seen as having a vertical or spiritual dimension, dignity, and purpose. In varying degrees, all created beings (trees, mountains, human beings, and so on) are meant to be God-connected— that is, finite glorifications of God. All beings and events, in other words, are in some fashion the enfleshments of God's redemptive activity. Edwards makes it very clear that it is in the life, death, and resurrection of Jesus Christ that God finally accomplishes God's redemptive work in its fullness. However, God's redemptive work has a larger scope. Jesus Christ is the climax and the center in God's redeeming work, but "lesser" though real salvations did occur before Jesus and are continuing to occur after Jesus. The scope of Jesus Christ's significance, in other words, is cosmic and everlasting—that is, theocentric. In such a theological perspective, all things and all events are, at least potentially, redemptive. Edwards' theocentric perspective makes the sanctification of the world the primary agenda in God's activity in the world. Our redemption is not for its own sake but rather for the greater and thus for the truly ultimate purpose of God's glorification of God's own being in time and history. The Reformed emphasis upon sanctification as inseparably connected with justification is particularly lifted up in the American theological tradition.

2. *God's own being is internally (not just externally) related to the world, thereby making temporal existence important to God's own life.* One of Jonathan Edwards' theological achievements was his attempt to see the divine being both as infinitely perfect in actuality and goodness and at the same time as "really" (i.e., in a way that matters to God) involved in the created world. Edwards attempted to find a genuine alternative to the God-world dualism of the traditional theism, on one hand, as well as to the almost complete temporalization of God (as in process thought), on the other.[8] For Edwards, God is essentially a sovereign and absolutely

perfect disposition of true beauty (self-giving love). This dis-
positional essence of the deity is fully actualized within
God's internal trinitarian relationships; thus, God is already
actually God. But God remains a disposition, and now seeks
to exercise God's essence externally—that is, in time and
space. What follows is God's creation of the world in and
through which God is repeating or multiplying God's internally actualized beauty, this time in time and space. The
world is to be a repetition of God's inner glory.

What this means is that the world is meant to be a temporal "embodiment" ("sacrament") of God's own life. Edwards'
own term is "type"—that is, a symbol that not only represents but also participates in and embodies that to which it
points. Trees, childbirths, and families—all things in creation are intended to be and can be, in varying degrees, the
finite and yet real "types" or embodiments of God's inner
glory.

But all creation is fallen. How, then, do created things
become embodiments of God's glory? Edwards' answer is
trinitarian and Christ-focused, and humanity plays a key
role vis-à-vis nature. God the Creator now works as the Redeemer and manifests God's true beauty in the history of
Israel but supremely in Jesus Christ so that the regenerate
minds and hearts can appreciate God's inner beauty and
again fulfill their ultimate end—namely, as embodiments of
God's inner glory. The Holy Spirit works within and through
human minds and hearts so that they may truly see and
become embodiments themselves of the divine beauty incar-
nate in Jesus Christ. What happens to the physical universe?
Its destiny to embody God's glory is achieved when the regenerate human beings with their divinely transformed
imaginations perceive the physical universe as the "images
or shadows of divine things."[9] God's redemptive history in
Jesus and in the history of Israel, as recorded in the Scriptures, functions as the "spectacles" or lenses (to use Calvin's
terminology) through which God's manifestations of God's
glory can be truly perceived and thus realized.

Faith then can be defined as involving a person's knowledge and love of God's beauty in Jesus Christ—the kind of knowledge and love that is accompanied by an active disposition to participate in God's ongoing creative-redemptive work: namely, God's glorification of God's own being in creation.

THE FAMILY AS A "TYPE" OF GOD'S BEAUTY

In the Edwardsian version of the Reformed theology, the order of creation cannot be sharply contrasted to the order of redemption. God's creative and providential activities are for the purpose of redemption. Edwards admits that redemption in its more limited sense refers to what God did in Jesus Christ. But when redemption is taken "more largely,"[10] it refers to all of God's providential activities before and after God's incarnation in Jesus. This is so because the very end for which God created and continues to sustain all things is that everything be a "type" or temporal and spatial embodiment of God's inner beauty, the meaning of that beauty having been clarified chiefly in the self-giving love of God in Jesus Christ.

In this perspective, the family as a part of the order of creation must be viewed as having been intended to be an embodiment of the divine self-giving love itself. It can be a "type" of the divine beauty. Even in the distorted realities of the families in their actual condition, we still see some traces of what they can be. I am aware of the alienation, conflicts, and pain that can and often do exist in family life as it empirically exists. Nevertheless, the human family still retains the important function of providing unconditional fidelity and caring—a remnant that points to its God-given destiny and its ultimate nature. There is present even in today's family, in other words, an indication of its potential as a "type" of God's self-giving love. The affectional function of the family is its essential function not only from the sociological perspective but also from our theological standpoint. Is it not precisely at this point that the religious destiny and significance of the family can still be discerned?

It is still in the family, for all its faults and problems, that human beings often stand by each other "regardless of what." It is still very often in the family that persons, especially children, learn to know that they are "somebody" in an unconditional way. It is in the faces of loving parents that infants first encounter enduring love and learn to have confidence in life. In short, the family even in its "fallen" condition, still retains traces of its destiny to be a "type" or embodiment of God's self-giving love and thus its God-given potential to participate in and also express the order of redemption.

As we turn to the Bible, we find there the story of God's redemptive work told as God's gathering of a radically new community of God's people, "the family of God." The new community of radical obedience and loyalty is portrayed in familial language, thereby affirming the religious significance of the human family as a "type" or embodiment of God's glory. At the same time, the new "family of God" embraces radically new dimensions in terms of which the "fallen" family as well as the sinful individual will need to be transformed. What we must carefully note here is that the new order of things points to the true fulfillment, not the displacement, of God's fallen creation, including the family. The new reality of "the family of God" does not abrogate the religious significance of the human family but rather reaffirms and restores it.

So, God calls and gathers together the community of faith, the new "ethnos," in and through which God's intention for the whole human race is accomplished here on earth. And the Bible portrays this new ethnos as a new family, "the household of God" (Eph. 2:19). God begins to build this new community by calling Father Abraham and Mother Sarah to the life of a radically new obedience and confidence. "Go from your country and your kindred and your father's house to the land that I will show you" (Gen. 12:1). And God promises that "by you all the families of the earth shall bless themselves" (Gen. 12:3). This building of the new "household of God" is climaxed through the work of Jesus Christ; the words in 1 Peter 2:9–10 declare the radical new reality "in Christ," "the family of God":

> But you are a chosen race, a royal priesthood, a holy nation, God's own people, that you may declare the wonderful deeds of him who called you out of darkness into his marvelous light. Once you were no people but now you are God's people; once you had not received mercy but now you have received mercy.

We must note, first of all, the biblical and especially Christ's own use of the family as the symbol for the redeemed order of life. Jesus himself announces the astounding good news of salvation by calling the almighty God his "abba." Jesus, by enduring the suffering on the cross, exhibits the costly and unconditional graciousness of God's self-giving love because of which all men and women may also call God their own "abba."[11] As has been pointed out, the inner-trinitarian life of God's own being is described in familial symbolism. Ephesians 5 compares the relationship between Christ and the church to the relationship between husband and wife. As John H. Elliott has forcefully pointed out in his recent commentary on 1 Peter, the redeemed community of the first-century Christians is portrayed in terms of the very concrete reality of "household" (oikos).[12] Human family, in spite of its present fallen condition, is a symbol of the divine act of grace.

The other side of the biblical message about the new family of God is its radical newness. And its radical character consists in three elements: (1) the absolute and single-hearted loyalty to the God whom Jesus called "abba"; (2) the formation of genuine human community with the new knowledge and love of the self-giving God as its basis; and (3) the radical inclusiveness in the scope of the community.

The point in Jesus' statements about the family is the disciples' single-hearted loyalty to the God of love and justice, rather than an abolishment of the human family. "Who are my mother and my brothers?" Jesus answered his own question: "Here are my mother and my brothers! Whoever does the will of God is my brother, and sister, and mother"

(Mark 3:33–35). The message in the following very strong statement, I believe, is again about the Christian's fundamental revolution in his or her loyalties:

> For I have come to set a man against his father, and a daughter against her mother, and a daughter-in-law against her mother-in-law; and a man's foes will be those of his own household. He who loves father or mother more than me is not worthy of me; and he who loves son or daughter more than me is not worthy of me. (Matt. 10:35–37)

Abraham was called to demonstrate the same radical loyalty to God through the sacrifice of his son Isaac. But as we know, his son was given back to him by the God to whom Abraham was absolutely faithful. Jesus too calls for a transvaluation of our usual values, including our values about the human family. But Jesus often showed his reaffirmation of the relative and still God-given value of the human family. He blessed the marriage feast of Cana. He indicated that marriage partners were "joined together" by God (Mark 10:9). One of the most moving portrayals Jesus gave about the unconditionally loving character of God was in terms of an unfailingly loving father and his wandering son (Luke 15:-11–32). Jesus acted out God's love for "God's children" by telling his own disciples to "let the children come to me" (Matt. 19:14).

The new family of God is also a genuine human community where one now even loves his or her own enemy. The radically new mutuality of this "body of Christ" is exemplified by the community of the first-century Christians as recorded in the book of Acts. This new community is, finally, radically inclusive. Jesus himself eloquently acted out this inclusiveness by befriending persons of all backgrounds and all kinds of reputation, including reputable persons like Nicodemus and not so reputable people like Zacchaeus. Paul transmits the same spirit in Galatians: "In Christ Jesus you are all sons of God, through faith. . . . There is neither Jew nor Greek, there is neither slave nor free, there is neither male nor female; for you are all one in Christ Jesus" (Gal.

3:26–28). All this is summed up in the following words:
"Once you were no people but now you are God's people."
"Beloved, we are God's children now" (1 Peter 2:10; 1 John
3:2).

We may now ask: Does the family of God consist only of
graciously transformed human families? Do human beings
become members of the family of God only as families or also
as single persons? Does the family of God include only married persons or also unmarried individuals? How important
is the natural human family (as kinship system) for the
family of God?

We put the questions in the above manner because they
are usually posed in that way. But perhaps we should distinguish the issues of marriage and family. Jesus himself and
also the apostle Paul were not married. Thus, it can be in-
ferred that marriage certainly may *not* be a requirement for
membership in the family of God. But Jesus and also Paul
surely belonged to their own natural human families (kinship relationships) at least during a portion, especially the
earlier part, of their lives. And it cannot be denied that their
early family life might have been a crucial influence upon
their entire life. For this reason, the questions of marriage
and of family are at least distinguishable, if not separable.

So, people become members of the family of God not only
as married persons but also as unmarried individuals.
Nevertheless, this does not deny the fundamental importance of the natural human family in the economy of God's
creation and redemption. The biblical use of the familial
symbolism for the nature of God and also of the redeemed
community testifies to this assertion. And the placement of
the family in the order of creation does not separate it from
the order of redemption. As we have seen, the human family
is intended by God to be an embodiment or "type" of God's
own glory in this life and in this history. Human family can
participate in and also exhibit the reality of the redeemed
life of the family of God. It would be natural to conclude,
then, that all the members of the family of God, married or
single, have as a part of their vocation the task of helping to

strengthen the natural human family. Persons living in their kinship system have the calling of making their family life more faithfully a "type" or embodiment of the glory of God. Persons in the family of God who are no longer living in their natural kinship setting also have as their vocation the responsibility to help natural families become true embodiments of God's self-giving love.

THE FAMILY, ITS SINS AND ITS TRANSFORMATION

We began this essay with an outline of a theocentric outlook according to which the entire creation is intended to be the temporal embodiment of God's inner life of self-giving love. It was then suggested that the affectional function of the supposedly "weakened" family may indeed be the family's essential function and also a trace of its ultimate religious significance—that is, its destiny to become an earthly embodiment of God's inner life. We then looked at the biblical account of God's gathering of the new redeemed community, the family of God. This radically new reality reaffirms the religious significance of the human family as a potential participant in God's redemptive work. But, at the same time, the reality of the family of God judges the empirical family as fallen from its God-intended destiny and thus in need of restoration and transformation.

We must now briefly explain the nature of the sinfulness of the human family in its affectional function and also indicate the various ways in which the family may be transformed so that it may truly embody, and participate in, the new reality of the family of God.

For my purpose, I will adopt Herbert Anderson's definition of the "purposes of the family" and use it to discuss the various modes of the family's affectional function: that is, procreation, social stability (socialization, community), and individuation.[13] Anderson's definition of the family itself as a "kinship system" (a definition that we also adopted earlier in this essay) entails its procreative function either through natural birth or by other means such as adoption. This procreative function attaches to the family an element of inevitability; everyone is dependent upon the family in this way. It is also within the family that children learn to relate to other human beings; the family is the most basic locus for human socialization. This process of socialization also makes individuation possible. The support and fidelity of family members enable individuals to become "autonomous," that is, capable of going beyond the natural family to the larger world as confident and self-respecting persons.

The human race is fallen, however. That is to say, families do fulfill, in varying degrees, their natural functions; but they do so in ways that are infected by idolatry, self-centeredness, and greed. "Turning in on itself" is the crux of the sinfulness not only of individuals but also of families. The slogan "Families that pray together stay together" involves an attitude of setting up the family as an end in itself. "Taking care of one's own," a noble motive in itself, can, however, turn a family away from the larger world. Individualism in its various forms is very much present in today's family life. E. David Willis describes the privatized family in vivid language:

> Without some sense of calling as a family to a higher cause beyond itself, a family easily becomes sticky and suffocating. Mother love becomes smother worry, father love becomes patriarchal authoritarianism, childhood becomes consumer tyranny, brotherhood and sisterhood become boot-camp training for the battle of the sexes.[14]

Speaking from my own Asian-American context, the Asian emphasis upon family and thus the relational character of human existence, I believe, is often a healthy alternative to the excessive individualism in Western culture. Asian teenagers do not leave home when they go to college, as most American teenagers tend to assume. However, the Asian emphasis upon family at times goes too far. In the immigrant situation, where children are heavily influenced by American individualism and parents are protective of their cultural roots, many severe and often tragic conflicts erupt between the generations. Asian immigrant parents need to examine their absolutization of family, while their children would benefit from a more critical assessment of American individualism.

So, all the functions of the family become infected by sin. Having children, through birth or adoption, often becomes a means to the self-perpetuation and self-extension of the parents' own selves. The process of nurturing for socialization often becomes an indoctrination of selfish, idolatrous, and privatistic values. Families often fail in helping children become autonomous individuals because of the lack of an appreciation for individual differences. In these and many other ways, the human family is in need of transformation. The affectional function which is a natural and God-given opening or potential for the family's becoming an embodiment of God's love is crying out to be restored and fulfilled.

Please note that we have used the term "sin" as the root problem of human families in their present condition. The fundamental nature of the problems of the family, as well as of human individuals, is not merely psychological, sociological, medical, political, or economic. The basic problem is religious: namely, a break in the relationship between human families (and family members) *and* their Creator. Faith or the transformation of their entire orientation toward their Creator and by implication toward their neighbors is what is called for.

Faith, as we mentioned earlier, can be defined as a person's, and a family's, knowledge and love of the self-giving fidelity of God in Jesus Christ with the accompanying active disposition to embody in their lives, and also to participate in, the new divine community of self-giving love. When families attain faith, they become faith-families and integral members of the new redeemed community, the family of God. Faith-families become the earthly embodiments of the divine familial community of the Holy Trinity.

How can we describe some of the marks of a faith-family? We may use here the three characteristics of the family of God as a measure of the human family's faithfulness to its

God-given destiny: (1) an absolute loyalty to and confidence in the beauty of the self-giving God in Christ; (2) the building of a genuine community of fidelity and mutuality; and (3) radical inclusiveness in the scope of its concern and care. Let us briefly outline how each of the three affectional functions of the family in its fallen condition will need to be transformed.

Procreation

A faith-family now has a purpose beyond itself or its members in the acts of procreation and of nurturing. Let it be made clear that having children is in no way a requirement for a disciple of Christ. Children are not a necessity for salvation but rather the gifts of God. And when children do come, either by birth or by adoption, it is the Christian vocation for their parents or parent to provide them with a home where they can experience God's love.

Thus, having children is not to be a vocation for every Christian. When a Christian couple are capable of having children, either by birth or by adoption, their decision to have them or not to have them cannot but be affected by the wider horizon of concerns that they now have as Christians. In the overpopulated parts of the world, a family that is mindful of the well-being of the larger community may naturally think twice about having a large number of children.

In technologically developed countries, however, married couples may be in need of regaining a sense of purposiveness and hope in the work of giving birth. Some adults today seem to have lost interest in having children, either because of their preoccupation with their individual fulfillment or because of a basic uncertainty about the future of human history itself. Married couples who are members of the family of God would no longer think only of their own individual ambitions but would also be willing to broaden their circles of love and care by welcoming the vocation of rearing children with joy and gratitude—assuming, of course, that their circumstances permit this task. Further, the members of the redeemed community live with a vibrant confidence in the ultimate triumph of God's will in human history.[15] They bring future generations of the family of God into the world with hope and trust. Moved by the inclusive vision of God's care for humanity, Christian adults would also be mindful not only of the well-being of their own families as genuine communities of love but also of the needs of many children in the world who have no home or have inadequate care at their own homes.

Socialization

The family is the usual place where children learn to find significant others and also gain a communal base. Christian families have not only their own resources for mutual love and caring; they are moved to love by the transcendent and unconditional graciousness of God in Christ. Daniel Day Williams has identified five characteristics of authentic love: a respect for individuality, an acknowledgment of each other's freedom, a willingness to act and suffer on behalf of each other always with persuasiveness instead of with coercion, and a rational and "objective" care in "discovering" the needs of the other.[16] However we define the nature of genuine human caring, the human family is a primary grouping in society where love needs to be practiced.

The task of building a communal base for an individual also involves the establishment of family traditions and rituals, the telling of stories, and the nurturing of common histories. But Christian families must avoid an exclusive inward direction or privatization of their life together. Families must transmit to their future generations not only their own stories but also the story of the God of Israel and of Jesus of Nazareth. And the stories of other people and other cultural worlds also need to be told. As H. Richard Niebuhr once pointed out, the followers of Christ must become "immigrants" into the "empire of God" which extends into the histories and parts of all peoples and all cultures.[17]

Speaking again about my own Asian immigrant context,

the first generation must stop clinging only to their own
cultural past and must be willing to enter into their newly
adopted world, the American society. The second generation
should avoid an idolatrous worship of "the American way of
life" and also learn to remember their parents' roots with
respect and appropriate pride. Immigrants are called to
move into the wilderness in search of that "city which has
foundations, whose builder and maker is God" (Heb. 11:10).
The community-building in a Christian family not only
seeks its own solidarity (which it needs to build) but reaches
out to the whole world. In Asian immigrant homes, where
two cultures meet and often conflict, the reaching out is
essential precisely for the building of their solidarity. They
cannot simply be Asian anymore, nor can they be "white
American." They need to build a new self-identity as Asian-
Americans. If this pilgrim task fails, Asian immigrant
homes will not be able to fulfill their function as the place
of nurturing and socialization for their children who live on
the cultural boundary. May I dare to add that Anglo-Ameri-
cans (as well as Americans with other racial and ethnic
backgrounds) also must reach out beyond their own cultural
worlds if they are to live as the members of the family of God
and if they themselves are to function faithfully as a place
for socialization of their children in a culturally diverse
world.

Individuation

Families exist not only for community but also for the
individuation of their members. The human family is the
primary agent in society where persons grow in their confidence as particular selves capable of moving into the larger
world. Families, therefore, need to learn "to let their children go" as well as to continue to be a place where they can
always return.

It is in this area of individuation that a balance of what
Paul Tillich called the "polarity of individuation and participation" is particularly crucial.[18] My observation is that

Asian families tend to overemphasize the participation side of the polarity (the family belongingness), while American families are inclined exactly in the opposite direction.[19] Many American youth seem to think they must (and they do) leave home and become completely autonomous agents when they leave for college. Asian immigrant families often refuse to accept that their children need to be individuals as well as someone's sons and daughters. A balance in this area is impossible, from a Christian theological point of view, unless both parents and their children find an ultimate sense of peace and acceptance in the transcendent self-giving love of God in Christ. Autonomy (individuality) and heteronomy (community) cannot achieve a balance without theonomy (participation in the family of God).

Further, a Christian family helps its children become individuals not only for their individual fulfillment or successes. The Christian family has the God-given vocation to nurture individuals who will live with a vision and concern for the whole of humanity. When families have their babies baptized, they covenant with God that their children may grow to be loyal not only to themselves or to their families but above all to the reign of God's love in the world. The members of the congregation, a part of the family of God, also covenant with the families and their children to provide the concrete and continuing support to those children as well as to their families. Without this covenant, infant baptism is not only ineffectual but is emptied of its essential meaning. The vision of the congregation in their ministry with and for the families and their children also must have an inclusive and global outlook, not only a concern for the well-being of individual families or individual congregations.

A WORD ABOUT FAMILIES AND THE CHURCH

Our basic thesis has been this: The family in its affectional function (a function that is its most essential power and that makes it indispensable to society) is created to become an active participant in, as well as an earthly embodiment of, God's redemptive activity in the world when it is itself redeemed from its fallenness and is grafted into the new reality of the family of God.

How, then, is the church related to families? We may simply draw some implications from what we have said thus far. First of all, the human family has a religious destiny as well as a social function. The family's affectional function is its potential to participate in God's ongoing creative-redemptive activity. The family's problems are, therefore, fundamentally religious; the family, in fulfilling its affectional function, is in need of being redeemed from sin and in need of being empowered by God's Spirit. When the church ministers to families through Word, Sacrament, and caring service, the church is helping the family to fulfill not simply its human or social roles but also its religious and theocentric destiny. Faith is relevant to today's families on the most fundamental level possible. That human families become earthly embodiments of God's own glory is important to God's own life.

Second, if the church is the community of redeemed persons, then the families, when they are transformed into embodiments of God's love by God's grace, are integral parts of the church. Within the theological perspective delineated in this essay, the family as a part of the order of creation cannot be considered only as a passive object of the church's redemptive ministry. Creation is not simply a backdrop for redemption but rather is itself intended for redemption. Creation is itself fulfilled in and through redemption. The family's destiny is to be a "little" redeemed community and also a redeeming "means of grace."

On the one hand, the church cannot exist without faith-families. It is true that in a sense people join the church as individuals. But people also join the church as members of families. To the extent that all human individuals, married or single, are initially nurtured in a family, the church cannot exist without families. Further, if the affectional function or the stable and loving nurture of children is an essen-

tial function of the family and if this function becomes a
vehicle of the communication of God's self-giving love, then
the family can be the indispensable nurturing place of faith.
In these ways, the faith-family can be *an active agent* in the
church's work of the proclamation of the gospel.

At the same time, however, the family as it often exists
needs the ministry of the church. Families need to be transformed by the good news of God's gracious act of redemption
in Jesus Christ, and the church must faithfully fulfill its role
of proclaiming that good news in word and in deed.

This is another way of saying that the church's first responsibility vis-à-vis the family is to *be* the church—that is,
a true family of God. And this the church must be not only
in word but especially in deeds. Members of the church,
married or single, old or young, have a high responsibility to
extend support and care to individual families and their
members especially when certain families are having difficulties in fulfilling their affectional function and also when
certain individuals are without the support of a family.
Through such acts of love, members of the church communi-
cate God's transforming grace to families and individuals.

In this way, we do not endorse a view that would affirm the
family's "natural" ability to function as little redemptive
communities, nor do we accept a dualistic conception in
which families belong only to the order of creation and not
to the realm of redemption. Families are fallen and in need
of redemption. But as they are transformed by God's grace
and incorporated into the family of God, they can be little
redeeming communities.

Thus, we can still affirm the basic intent of what Jonathan
Edwards wrote over two hundred years ago:

> Every Christian family ought to be as it were a little church
> consecrated to Christ, and wholly influenced and governed by his
> rule. And family education and order are some of the chief means
> of grace. If these fail, all other means are likely to prove ineffec-
> tual. If these are duly maintained, all the means of grace will be
> likely to prosper and be successful.[20]

6

Family Promises: Faith and Families in the Context of the Church

Craig Dykstra

What is essential to being family? What connections are there between family and Christian faith? And what do our answers to these two questions suggest about church and family, and about Christian education in relation to church and family? These are the questions before us. I want to suggest that good answers emerge when we recognize that, more than anything else, promises are central to being family.

There are a number of ways of understanding what a family is, all of them useful from one point of view or another. But one way that is particularly helpful, both because it says something about what is essential to the nature of all families—just as families—and because it helps us to make a fundamental connection between families and faith, focuses on the promissory nature of the family. Families are people who make *promises* to each other. When we see what those promises are, we see what a family is. It is important to be clear on what is being suggested here. I am not saying that first there is a family, and then those who are that family start making promises. What I mean, rather, is that family is *constituted* by promises. "Family" *is* a peculiar set of promises. It is the promises that make the family, before it is the family that makes promises.

A fairly common sense definition of "family" runs as follows: "Family" is that group of persons with whom we are linked as parents or children or siblings or spouses or kin, by birth, by adoption, or by marriage. This definition suggests that virtually every person is part of a family—unless, of course, one has no kin at all. It does not by any means limit "family" to a married couple and their children. Never married and formerly married people are part of families, whether they have children or not. Married couples without children are in family. People who live alone are almost always still in families. "Family" does not mean "people living together under one roof." If people have parents, sisters, brothers, children, uncles, aunts, nieces, nephews, or cousins, and so forth, they are in family. "Family" is a very inclusive category when the tracings of kinship are brought to our attention and our imaginations are not limited by stereotypes.

Still, this definition, standing by itself, does not tell us much about what family *means*. The crucial phrase in the definition is "we are linked." But what is the nature of this linkage? Is it simply biological or sociological? Or is something deeper implicit in all of this? In order to ferret this out, we need to ask what these words "parent," "children," "spouse," and "kin" really mean. Here is where the notion of promise-making comes in. It helps us to see what is at the heart of being linked.

Marriage is not, of course, the only way to be and become family. But if we start with marriage, we find a fairly clear way to open up the promise-making nature of all kinds of family constellations. How do people get married? How does a person become a husband or a wife? It is by making a promise, by saying "I promise . . ." or "I take thee . . ." or "I will . . ." or "I do." That is it. An act of promising constitutes the marriage. It, in and of itself, creates a family. To be a spouse, to be a wife or a husband in relation to someone else, means nothing else but to have made some promises.

What are people doing when they make promises like this? In an act of promise-making, people are saying something about their intentions for the future. They are committing themselves to a particular way of moving through the present into the future. This is what it means to make a promise. And what is it that people are promising here in the act of marrying? To what particular way of moving through the present into the future are they committing themselves? The most fundamental promise is this: henceforth to see the other *as spouse,* as wife to me or husband to me. This means a number of things. It means mutual acceptance of responsibility for each other's welfare. It means commitment to work out together, as husband and wife, the financial, personal, cultural, and social problems that arise in life. It means to see each other and both together as the human matrix of whatever children may come from the sexual relationship, and to take mutual responsibility for them. To see another as spouse means seeing the other in terms of a future that involves mutual responsibility in sexuality, in sustenance, and in dealing with realities and forces that impinge on the lives of each of us.[1] All of this is involved in "meaning" each other as a spouse. A family comes into being when two persons become spouse to each other (and are seen as spouse to each other by others) through a public act of promising.

The case of the formation of a family through marriage as an act of promising is probably the clearest case. Can we think of other relationships in family in the same way? Do we become parents, daughters and sons, brothers and sisters, grandparents, aunts, uncles, and cousins through making promises? In these cases the matter is not nearly so clear, since there seems to be no explicit act of promise-making involved and the causes seem more biological than anything else. Still, a strong case can be made that all of the various relationships that make us kin or family are constituted ultimately in promising.[2]

Ordinarily, we tend to think that the paradigmatic case of the establishment of the parent-child relationship is the one in which the child is biologically born from the union

of the parents. But if promising is really at the heart of
being family, then the process of adoption may offer a better example. When people adopt children, they do something similar to what is done in marrying. They say, in a
sense, "I promise" in answer to the question, "Will you
take this child to be your son or daughter?" In saying "I
promise" (or "We promise"), people are promising henceforth to see this child, "mean" this child, as son or daughter
to them. Again, to see a child as son or daughter involves
implicit (if not explicit) intentions to live out the future in
a particular way that includes commitment to and responsibility for the child's welfare, identity, and future. And it
means that it is *as father* or *as mother* that they shall
carry out these commitments and responsibilities to the
child *as son* or *as daughter.*

When a person adopts a child, this promise-making is
fairly explicit. Adopting parents have to make certain particular promises publicly and explicitly to adoption agencies
(and have their fitness for making those promises checked up
on and tested out) before they are allowed to adopt. The
promise-making involved when children issue out of our own
bodies is not as obvious. But it is no less the case. We make
promises, I think, whenever we engage in sexual intercourse
—whether we know it or not. An act of promise-making is
occasioned by this sexual act. Ronald Green, in an essay on
the ethics of abortion called "Abortion and Promise-Keeping," argues as follows:

> The mere fact that coitus, when followed by conception, initiates
> a series of events that normally culminates in a set of legitimate
> expectations on the part of another human being (the future
> child) places the individual who has helped initiate that act
> . . . under particular obligation to fulfill those expectations.
>
> Precisely because these expectations have an objective basis,
> we contend that any [person] capable of understanding the im-
> plications of coitus must eventually realize the promise-making
> nature of [his or] her sexual acts. Thus, we are not so much saying
> that a promise is *implicitly made* as that a promise is *implicit to*
> this act.[3]

Sexual intercourse is in and of itself implicitly promissory. Just by having intercourse, we make promises to any potential offspring of that action.[4] If a child is conceived, he or she *becomes* son or daughter to us (whether we like it or not) precisely through the promises implicit in our act. The promissory nature of family which arises from children biologically born to us is no different from the promissory nature of family constituted through adoption. Here too we "promise" henceforth to be father or mother to sons or daughters.

What about from the other side? Do children make promises to be sons and daughters? Or to be brothers and sisters? Such an idea seems odd, at the very least. Children have mothers, fathers, sisters, and brothers through no choice of their own. From the point of view of the offspring, no volition is involved. None of us chooses even to be born, much less to be born into the particular family we are given. How can any promising be involved in being a son or daughter, a brother or sister?

Here the promises are even more implicit and arise out of receiving and responding to the promises made to us by our parents. In being parents to children, parents engage their children in an ever-developing web of mutuality. This mutuality is founded initially, to be sure, on the promises of the parents. But in responding to those promises, children implicitly make promises back. To be seen as daughter or as son by one's father or mother evokes the response on the child's part of seeing oneself *as* son or daughter and, reciprocally, the parent or parents *as* mother or father. The reciprocal seeing has implicit in it a reciprocal promising. This is experienced quite powerfully at a rather early age. But it is only later that these promises may become explicitly conscious to the child; and even later still, perhaps, that they may be intentionally owned.[5] Nevertheless, at the point where the child's promises become conscious and owned, there are not promises newly being made. Rather, the promises are existing, already-lived promises becoming articulated and affirmed (or, perhaps, rejected).

This same kind of process goes on in making us brothers

and sisters in families. Parents see *all* their children as their sons or daughters. As children see their parents seeing them and the other children in the family as all being their children (in short, as brothers and sisters), each child comes to see herself or himself that way too. That is, each child comes to see himself or herself as incorporated *with* the other children in the family into that particular set of promises which constitutes the family. The same kind of analysis can be made in relation to more distant kin, though in such cases (especially in some cultures such as our own) the promises quickly become much more restricted and the opportunities for seeing other kin at all—much less *as kin*—diminishes rapidly.

The purpose of all of this is simply to make clear the claim that families—all families, not just Christian families or families in the church—are constituted most fundamentally by promises. Families are people who make a particular set of promises to each other. How this illumines the relationship of "family" to Christian faith and to the church and to Christian education is what we are moving toward. But to get there, a few other things must be said first.

One thing that must be said is this: it is promise-*making,* not promise-*keeping,* that constitutes the family. As a matter of fact, the promises that constitute the family are very difficult promises to keep, and we all continually fail at doing so. We fail for all sorts of reasons. We may fail because certain cultural, social, and economic forces quite beyond our control make it extremely difficult, if not impossible, for us to fulfill our promises to promote each other's welfare, to work out problems and difficulties mutually, to attend to each other as husband, wife, father, mother, daughter, son, sister, or brother. War, poverty, racism, sexism, societal violence, pornography, dislocation are all powerful forces that make our promise-keeping difficult to fulfill and sometimes impossible. Or we may fail because of our human limitations. Often the promises involved in being family are too many and too overwhelming for us to fulfill, just because there are limits to our energy and to our capacities to know and see and be in the ways that the fulfillment of our promises would require. Or, again, our failure may be due to our own sinfulness: our deceiving, insincerity, manipulation, idolization, ridiculing, and self-centeredness.

It is not the failure to keep promises, in and of itself, that destroys family. Such failure happens in every family and can be expected. Family can remain family in the midst of unfulfilled promises. What destroys family is the collapse of promise-*making.* It is when the very making of promises is no longer believed and believed in that families die. The failure to keep promises and the collapse of promise-making are, of course, related. The continual failure to fulfill promises acts as a corrosive to the promise-making, so that there may come a time when the lack of fulfillment destroys the very meaning and significance of promise-making. But when this happens, it is the promise-making itself that becomes null and void. Then the constituting ground of family is dissolved. In divorce, for example, a certain set of promises are no longer being made. The promise-making that constitutes two persons as husband and wife comes to an end. That is what makes them no longer husband and wife.

CHRISTIAN FAITH AND FAMILY PROMISES

As we have seen, many of the promises that are involved in the constitution of family are somewhat hidden and implicit. It is not obvious what promises we are making when we marry or have children or just find ourselves to be kin to someone. Because of this, it is very easy to marry, or have children, without knowing what we are doing—without knowing what promises we are making and without even knowing that we are making promises at all. This is all the more true as our culture becomes more secularized. In fact, one thing secularization may mean is the removal of the context and grounds for the visibility, significance, and meaning of promise-making.

Promises can be so slippery. So often in our lives we cannot tell whether we have been promised something or not. Suppose someone tells me, "I will be there." Has that person made a promise? It is an open question. It depends. It depends upon whether that person was just stating a hope or a wish or a reasonable expectation—or making a promise. We cannot always tell just from the words themselves. The words themselves are continually open to further questioning by all parties involved *unless* the words have been said in some context that secures them as a promise.

Richard Fenn, in a fascinating book entitled *Liturgies and Trials,* suggests that liturgies are those contexts which secure promises. He says that secure promises

> are rare in human conversation. When they occur, they are given and received with signs and symbols that something out of the ordinary is occurring. I am thinking specifically of wedding ceremonies in which extraordinary care is taken that all the conditions are fulfilled that make full-blown promises possible for mere humans. Announcements of intention to marry and a final pronouncement begin and conclude a process in which both persons promise that only death will part them. There can be no mistake about the seriousness of this promise, and its seriousness is guaranteed by those who watch with "the eyes of God" as rings are exchanged, hands clasped, and solemn steps taken. Even those who know of conditions that would prevent a full-blown promise from taking place are told to speak (now) or keep silent forever. The liturgical language of religion is therefore the last human defense against the slipperiness, ambiguity, and uncertainty of all human acts of speech; and even these liturgical guarantees are widely known to fail.[6]

Fenn is suggesting that a secular culture, a culture without liturgies that make promises secure by the promises of God, is a culture that allows our promise-acts continually to be open to question—and thus continually unstable. A radically secular culture is one in which no adequate context and grounds are provided for the visibility, significance, and meaning of promise-making.

What happens to marriage, childbearing and child-rearing, relationships between brothers and sisters, responsibilities of children to their parents—in short, to family—in a culture that fails to make implicit promises visible, significant, meaningful, and secure? What happens is that the promissory foundations that constitute family are undercut. In a radically secular context, divorce is not seen as grievous failure in the sacred matter of promise-making requiring confession, repentance, forgiveness, and the grace that is needed to make promises at all. It is simply the (perhaps sad and even painful) ending of one phase of two person's lives and thereby the beginning of another. What it requires is only readjustment.[7] Similarly, parents and children, brothers and sisters, come to be seen (and to see themselves) to be moving through stages of relationship in which everything may change from one stage to the next, nothing tying one stage to the next or each person to the other except a partly common past. The human task in such a situation is simply to cope and adjust. We can make no demands on one another or call one another to account. We cannot even cry out, "But you promised!"

Now we are at the point where we can come to see some of the crucial significance of the Christian faith for family. Two points are crucial. First, in the context of Christian faith, the promises that are constitutive of family are made conscious, public, and binding. Second, in this same context, these promises are linked with other similarly serious and binding, but wider, promises. The linkage of the family promises with these other promises deepens the significance of the family promises and to some extent transforms them, while at the same time providing support and empowerment for the fulfillment of the family promises.

One of the important ways in which the Christian faith makes conscious, public, and binding the promises that are central to the family is through its liturgies. Among the most obvious of the liturgies that deal with family is the marriage service. Let us take two Presbyterian liturgies as an example. In the 1946 edition of *The Book of Common Worship,* used for many years in Presbyterian churches, there is an "Order for the Solemnization of Marriage."[8] The idea of "solemnization" suggests that something very serious is going on and that it should be recognized as such, that what is going on has a dignity and form to it that need to be respected, and even that there is something sacred about what is taking place to which we are to respond with a sense of awe and humility.

In the service itself, all of this is made quite clear. The minister tells us that "we are assembled here in the presence of God" and that what is happening is "instituted of God, regulated by His commandments, blessed by our Lord Jesus Christ, and to be held in honor among all." Once this context is set, it is made very clear that promises are about to be given and received; and what those promises are is articulated. "By His apostles, [our Saviour] has instructed those who enter into this relation to cherish a mutual esteem and love; to bear with each other's infirmities and weaknesses; to comfort each other in sickness, trouble, and sorrow; in honesty and industry to provide for each other, and for their household, in temporal things; to pray for and encourage each other in the things which pertain to God; and to live together as the heirs of the grace of life." Then follows the question to all present as to whether there is any known impediment to the making of these promises. And then, as if to reinforce the seriousness of the matter, the persons to be married are charged to examine themselves. "I charge you both, before the great god, the Searcher of all hearts, that if either of you know any reason why ye may not lawfully be joined together in marriage, ye do now confess it. For be ye well assured that if any persons are joined together otherwise than as God's Word allows, their union is not blessed by Him."

After a prayer for God's blessing, but before vows are taken, the minister asks both of those to be married a question, the same question. The question is framed in such a way that the nature of the promises to be made is clearly stated. It asks, in essence, whether these persons know what they are doing and are ready to do it. And the minister expects and must get an answer before going on. "*N.*, wilt thou have this Woman (Man) to be thy wife (husband), and wilt thou pledge thy troth to her (him), in all love and honor, in all duty and service, in all faith and tenderness, to live with her (him), and cherish her (him), according to the ordinance of God, in the holy bond of marriage?" Each must answer: "I will."

Only then is it possible actually to make the promise. The nature of the promise has been articulated already, so in the vow the statement goes directly to the heart of the matter: "I, *N.,* take thee, *N.;* to be my wedded wife (husband); and I do promise and covenant; before God and these witnesses; to be thy loving and faithful husband (wife)." But it is not left to chance that the promise makers know how significant and binding this promise is. So the conditions are set out. This promise holds under all conditions: "In plenty and in want; In joy and in sorrow; In sickness and in health; As long as we both shall live."

I have taken us through this marriage service in order to show the kinds of promises that the church (not just Presbyterians) has thought basic to the constitution of family, and to illustrate the clarity with which they are articulated and the firmness with which they are made secure. One sees nothing like this is a secular ceremony. But it is interesting that I had to turn to the older *Book of Common Worship* to find this. In *The Worshipbook,* published in 1970, the liturgy is not called a solemnization, but "The Marriage Service"; and the nature of the promises and the seriousness of making them are not nearly so clearly spelled out.[9] The vows are these: "_____, I promise with God's help to be your faithful husband (wife), to love and serve you as Christ commands, as long as we both shall live." This vow still points to the heart of the matter and makes it binding. But little else in the liturgy articulates what this promise means and involves, or assures the seriousness of the parties making the promises. If the Presbyterian case is at all reflective of what has been going on in the liturgies of other denominations, this may well be an indication that even the church's marriage rituals have become a bit secularized, allowing questions to arise about the nature and seriousness of the promises constitutive of the family through what is *not* said.

There is something quite good about the marriage service in *The Worshipbook,* however, that is not made nearly so evident in the liturgy in *The Book of Common Worship.* It is the way it helps to put the marriage promises in the context of a set of larger promises. As an "order for the public worship of God," it places marriage not only in the context of prayer but also in the context of confession of sin and the declaration of God's mercy, the reading and hearing of lessons from the Old and New Testaments, and the interpretation of God's Word through preaching. Used rightly by the minister, this liturgy can help make clear the second dimension of the relationship between family promises and Christian faith; namely, that marriage in the context of Christian faith places promises that are constitutive of family in inseparable relationship to wider promises.

Marriage is not the only promissory act of Christian faith, nor the only one celebrated in liturgy. Christian faith is imbued with a promissory structure as a whole. This promissory structure is made especially clear, and is enacted anew for each new Christian, in the Sacrament of Baptism.

The Sacrament of Baptism begins with an announcement of the promises of God. In *The Worshipbook,* for example, it says:

> In Jesus Christ, God has promised to forgive our sins, and has joined us together in the family of faith which is his church. . . . In Jesus Christ, God has promised to be our Father, and to welcome us as brothers and sisters of Christ.

> Know that the promises of God are for you. By baptism, God puts his sign on you to show that you belong to him, and gives you Holy Spirit as a guarantee that, sharing Christ's reconciling work, you will also share his victory; that, dying with Christ to sin, you will be raised with him to new life.[10]

In response to these promises of God, the person to be baptized (or, in the case of the baptism of a child, the child's parents) makes his or her own corresponding promises: "Do you intend (your child) to be [Christ's] disciple, to obey his word and show his love?" And if the person being baptized is also being received as a communicant member of the church, the following promise is added: "Will you be a faithful member of this congregation, giving of yourself in every way, and will you seek the fellowship of the church wherever you may be?" These promises are then, in turn, responded to by the church through the particular congregation. The minister says: "Our Lord Jesus Christ ordered us to teach those who are baptized. Do you, the people of the church, promise to tell this new disciple *(this child)* the good news of the gospel, to help him (her) know all that Christ commands, and, by your fellowship, to strengthen his (her) family ties with the household of God?"[11]

What these rubrics make prominent are *(a)* the promissory nature of the whole set of relationships (including God, the individual, and the wider Christian community) involved in the Christian life, *(b)* the vocational character of the Christian life as discipleship, and *(c)* the church as the context for the living out of that vocation.

So, it is not just the family that is founded on promises. The Christian faith as a whole is, too. Promise-making runs straight through the Judeo-Christian tradition from beginning to end. Israel came into existence on the basis of God's covenants with (God's promises to) Israel. And Christians are understood as the people of the new covenant, the new promises made known in the life, death, and resurrection of Jesus Christ. Christian faith is belief in and trust of those promises and the God who makes them; and it is our response to those promises with corresponding promises of our own to God and to each other.

What God promises is, most simply put, our redemption and the redemption of the world. The apostle Paul describes the whole world as "groaning in travail" (Rom. 8:22). We live in a world shot through with patterns and powers of destruction, and we participate in them ourselves. Afraid of each other, we fight with each other or flee each other's presence. Afraid of ourselves, we deceive ourselves and make ourselves

out to be both more and less than we actually are. Afraid of
death, we try to secure ourselves—either with the use of
force, or more subtly through competitiveness, callousness,
forgetfulness, selfishness, self-protectiveness, deceitfulness,
depersonalization, manipulation, and ridicule. Afraid even
of God, we summon our powers against God or try to ignore
God. And we seem to have no power of our own to keep
ourselves from living in this way—in our families, in our
work life, with our friends and colleagues as much as with
our enemies. As much as we would do and be otherwise, we
cannot. Sooner or later, in one way or another, sometimes
not even knowing that this is what we are doing, we cry out.
We want to be *saved* from this way of living. We want,
because we need, *redemption.*

And, behold, this is what God has promised. This is what
God gives. Another way has opened up and is possible. We
are given the gift of salvation and are called to participate
in the redemptive and transforming way of life that God
makes possible for us. We are promised new life. The response of faith is the response that believes and accepts
God's promises, and in turn promises simply to participate
in that new way of life. This is the Christian vocation, the
vocation of discipleship. The most basic promise made in the
baptismal liturgies is the promise to be a disciple. "Do you
intend (your child) to be [Christ's] disciple, to obey his word
and show his love?" To be a disciple means nothing other
than to be one who follows Jesus into the new life (the new
way of life) that God promises and makes possible through
him.

The connection between the family promises and the baptismal promises is that the promises we make as family are
a distinctive set of promises through which, in part, we live
out our promise to be disciples. As Christians, we are to be
family in the mode of discipleship. We are to be family in the
context of following Jesus Christ into new life. That is what
we promise when we follow the path of being baptized *and*
being family in the church.

The way in which this connection in some ways intensifies

and transforms the family promises may not be obvious. The Christian vocation of discipleship means that we live our lives in a peculiar way. It is a way characterized by confession of sin and repentance to God, together with confession to and repentance in relation to each other; by the recognition of God's grace and forgiveness and reconciliation, accompanied by our own forgiveness of and reconciliation with each other; by prayer of thanksgiving and praise and intercession to God, which involves giving thanks and praise for each other under all circumstances as well as intercession for each other; and by being servants of God in the world, which includes serving each other in the family and serving the world together as family. All of these disciplines of the Christian life are very difficult; and in some ways they make family life more difficult. They place responsibilities on us as families and as individuals in our families that, outside the context of Christian faith, we would not see or take on. They may make us more vulnerable and require us to take risks, face conflicts, and endure sufferings—both within our families and as families—that we would otherwise ignore, flee, or never encounter. They also, however, bear the fruit and bring the joy of the Christian life and allow the family to participate in that.

Furthermore, even when, because of our finitude, our sin, or some tragedy, our family promise-making fails or comes to some end, our discipleship promises do not. When we divorce, for example, and we no longer make family promises to the one who had been our spouse, our discipleship promises to God in relation to our former husband or wife do not cease. We may not be called and committed any longer to marriage, but we are still called to a life of confession, repentance, forgiveness, reconciliation, prayer, and service with and in relation to that person. This holds not only when there are still children to be cared for, but even when there are not. We may no longer love a person as husband or wife, but we are still to love each other as children of God and face each other in these terms.

The baptismal promises, as responding promises to the

promises of God, open up one further dimension. In the baptismal liturgy, it is made clear that we are not only receiving God's promises and making our own in response. We are also being incorporated into the family of the church. We promise to be faithful members of a particular congregation and to seek the fellowship of the church wherever we may be. We also receive the promise of the people of the church to tell us the good news of the gospel, to help us know all that Christ commands, and to strengthen our *family* ties with the household of God. Thus, not only are our family promises broadened and transformed in such a way as to be incorporated into the family of the household of God. The family of which we are a part is broadened and transformed in such a way as to be incorporated into the family of the household of God.

One implication of seeing the connection between faith and family in these terms is that the particular sociological shape of one's own family has no primacy. Whether one is married or has never been married or was formerly married; whether one does not have children or has two children or ten children; whether one does not have sisters or brothers or has ten; has twenty-five cousins or none—this is not terribly significant. What is significant is the nature of our discipleship in the context of whatever kind of family we happen to be a part of and the nature of the discipleship of that family as a whole. Our discipleship can be exercised faithfully in any of a multitude of family constellations, and families of very diverse arrangement can themselves be faithful. What becomes normative is not the kind of family situation we are a part of but the way in which our baptismal promises are carried out in relation to whatever family situation we are in.

A second implication is that family promising is no longer merely private. Family promising is no longer something that is just between two or a few persons (the kinship family alone). When family promises are incorporated into our discipleship promises and the family itself is incorporated into the family of the household of God, our family promises and activities become the concern of the whole church. This means the end of any attitude that suggests "What I and my family do is our business and nobody else's." As Christians together, even though we are not kin, the character and quality of *my* family promise-making is *your* business too, just as these matters in *your* life are *my* business. We have a responsibility now for each other's family promises—the making and breaking of them, the fulfilling and the non-fulfilling of them. It is a responsibility that requires of us not only mutual concern, care, and support but also mutual instruction and even discipline in these matters. We have now both the freedom and the responsibility to be involved in each other's family life. This, of course, is not sanction for aggressive nosiness or a neurotic preoccupation with each other's situations and problems, and even less for vindictive judging of others. It is, instead, a call for the gracious and appropriate mutual pastoral care of one another—both individually and corporately—in families and as families.[12] The idea that we have such freedom and responsibility is quite different from the common secular assumptions.

CHURCH AND FAMILY

What does this understanding of faith and family mean for the family in relation to the church and the church in relation to the family? It means, in the first place, that we must stop thinking of church and family as two completely separate entities. We do this so often and so easily, usually without really intending to. We speak, for example, of the church's ministry to families, as if the church were a body of people who were not in one way or another participants in families (or even as if the church were an institution without people at all). Or we speak of what families can do in and for the church, as if the church were not made up of people in families.[13]

Rather than seeing families as one thing and the church as another, we must learn to see Christian people as participants simultaneously in the promise-making that constitutes church *and* in the promise-making that constitutes

other covenantal relationships—including the family relationships we have as daughters or sons, sisters or brothers,
mothers or fathers, or spouses. We must learn to see the
promises involved in all of these relationships as promises
that mutually affect one another, and the people who make
them as living out their one vocation of discipleship in all of
them.

Perhaps we can make this a little clearer by noting that
the promise-making involved in being church and the promise-making involved in being family are not the only promise-making webs of relationships we are involved in. Letty
Russell has helped us to think of the church in terms of
partnership. The church, she argues, is partnership with
God and partnership with others in participation in the redemptive activity of God.[14] Our task as Christians is to become the partners that we are called to be, not just in congregations but also in work relationships, in friendships, in
political activity, in teaching and learning—and in marriage
and kinship; in short, in all of the relationships involved in
human living. All of these contexts and relationships are
potential contexts for partnership. But they become partnerships only when they are put in the perspective of and are
worked out in relation to God's promises, "God's promised
future of justice, freedom, and wholeness."[15] It is on the basis
of God's promises and our promises in response that any
relationship becomes a partnership.

What this suggests is that we see family relationships as
one of those particular sets of relationships of which we are
a part; one that becomes, through the promises which constitute them in relation to the wider promises involved in
Christian faith, a set of distinctive and significant partnerships for us. Family is one of a number of partnerships that
is both within and a part of the larger partnership of the
church. It is one that can contribute to other partnerships
within that larger partnership. And it is one that can be
sustained, nurtured, and developed by the influence of other
partnerships within that larger partnership. Being a disciple
means participating in the redemptive activity of God in the

world. We do this, not as individuals isolated from one another, but in partnership. These partnerships are not to be separated. Church and family are not to be separated. Rather, our families are a distinctive partnership in which we are involved in our participation in the redemptive activity of God in the world as the church.

This understanding of church and family raises some issues concerning how to understand family and church. Does this mean that we are to understand the church as a "family of families" of which the kinship family is the basic unit? My answer would be "no." The church is not made up of "family pews." It is not a "household" as individuals *apart* from our being in kinship families, either. Rather, we are individuals who participate in a variety of promise-making relationships —including family. We are members of the household of God *as* members of families—as people who have made family promises as well as congregational promises. What makes the family a *distinctive* partnership for us is the distinctive way and the distinctive power that the family has in shaping our identities, values, and ways of living, and the distinctive call it makes on our affections (and antagonisms), the use of our time, and the channeling of our responsibilities. The family receives this distinctiveness primarily from our inevitable closeness to it, whether for good or for ill, biologically, economically, socially, and psychologically.

If families are not units of the church family but still distinctive partnerships for us in our participation in the redemptive activity of God, what does this mean for families of "mixed faiths"? Or for families in which some are Christians and others are not? Or for families in which the understandings of and commitments to participation in God's redemptive activity vary so significantly as to be a source of conflict that undercuts rather than sustains partnership? These days, the idea of "the Christian family" often seems more ideal than reality. What does this do to our family promises in relation to our baptismal promises? Letty Russell makes some comments about partnership that are particularly helpful in relation to this. She says:

> The commitment made in partnership is never one in which we
> can be sure we will be faithful. All relationships entered into by
> Christian are lived in the threefold tension of the "already, not
> yet" of the *eschaton*. We are *already partners* even before we
> know one another, because God has reached out to us in Jesus
> Christ and has reconciled us, making us partners of one another
> and God. But we are also always in the process of *becoming
> partners.* And this is very difficult. It involves partnerships where
> commitments are broken, and persons betrayed, as well as the
> few relationships where there are signs that partnership might
> be a possibility. And at the same time we live in the hope that
> *we will become partners,* when the provisional signs of *koinōnia*
> in this life are realized fully in God's promised future. We are all
> partners, yet we experience not only growth but decline as we
> search out ways of living now, as if our relationships were those
> of full partnership.[16]

All of our partnerships are weak and remain at least partially unfulfilled—in our families no less than elsewhere.
But in their weakness, they are sustained by the promises of
God. Further, the partnership of the family may be nurtured, developed, and sustained partly through the promissory relationships with others—within congregations, or in
friendship, work, educational, political, or other settings—
that individuals in families may have, either on their own or
together with spouses, sons, daughters, brothers, or sisters.
Our hope, as Christians, is that all of our partnerships may
ultimately be so interwoven and mutually enlivening that
each contributes to the other toward the common aim and
task of participation in the redemptive activity of God. This
is why the church historically has recommended, for instance, marriage between persons who are both Christian. It
can make this all somewhat less difficult. But the church
does not prohibit marriage outside the faith, because it
recognizes that in such marriage, too, redemptive partnerships can be formed.[17] Our task, in all circumstances of family life, is for each of us to live our family promises as part
of our own baptismal promises, participating there too as

fully as we can in the redemptive activity of God for the sake of the whole world.

When church and family are both understood as partnerships based on the promises of God and our own corresponding promises, we can see that the roles of church in relation to family are no different from what they are in relation to any other partnership, relationship, or activity. The roles of the church are liturgical, missionary, and educational. The church is people in partnership in the worship of God. In liturgy, God is praised, given thanks, confessed to, heard from, and responded to through our own promise-making and going out to fulfill our promises. In marriage liturgies, we in partnership with the whole church make promises in the context of the worship of God. In baptismal liturgies, we —including not only parents or a parent but also aunts and uncles, grandparents and friends, the various members of the particular congregation as sponsors, and, in some traditions, godparents—in partnership with the whole church make promises for ourselves (and for our children) in the context of the worship of God. In going out to fulfill these promises, we engage in the mission of the church. In partnership with the whole church, we—in congregations, in families, and in local, national, and global arenas of work, education, and politics—go out to carry on the caring, sustaining, and reforming activity that is crucial to participation in the redemptive activity of God. And for the sake of both worship and mission, we educate. We do the work of training and educating ourselves in order that we become able to see, understand, and participate ever more deeply, widely, and powerfully in our worship and mission.

CHRISTIAN EDUCATION, THE CHURCH, AND THE FAMILY

This is where Christian education comes in. Christian education is that particular task which we, in partnership with each other as the church, engage in to enable each other and the whole church to see, understand, and participate ever more deeply, widely, and powerfully in the redemptive activity of God. Through Christian education, the church equips the saints for their ministry.

There are several ways of thinking of the relationship of church partnerships (e.g., congregations, denominations, schools) to family partnerships in terms of education. Since the congregation is a central and crucial such "partnership," let us focus on that and simply list a number of the options.

1. The congregation may involve families as whole family units in learning together.
2. The congregation may bring families together with other families to teach and learn from each other.
3. The congregation may (through some appointed teachers) teach all or some family members about families and help them better to carry out their responsibilities in the family through this.
4. The congregation may assume that each family has certain responsibilities for the Christian education of family members and that the congregation has other responsibilities for the education of those family members, and provide resources and help for the family to carry out its educational role.
5. The congregation may make available certain resources for Christian education within families as supplementary to the congregation's overall educational program, but take the main responsibility for Christian education as its own.
6. The congregation may train some particular family members (parents, for example) to be responsible for the Christian education of the other members of their families (the children, for example) in some or many of the same areas that the congregation also takes responsibility for in other ways.
7. The congregation may leave Christian education entirely to family units without providing any resources or help.

8. The congregation may assume that families have no part to play in Christian education and carry out its educational work only with individuals, disregarding the family entirely.

This list is just a series of logical possibilities, some more realistic than others. It is rare that congregations intentionally leave Christian education entirely to the family (7) or that they disregard the family entirely (8)—though this latter too often comes close to describing what happens in practice. In any case, neither of these is a valid policy or practice.

The other options, however, are all real alternatives that have been and are being carried out in many contemporary congregations. And some have even been the focus of denominational policy. Option 4, for example, was the explicit policy of the United Presbyterian Church U.S.A. with its *Christian Faith and Life* curriculum. That is why it both carried out its work in the church school *and* provided so many resources for use in the home and for helping parents to teach in the home. Later, feeling that this approach had been for the most part a failure, it turned to option 5 as the major policy governing the Presbyterian *Christian Faith and Action,* supplementing that with some strategies along the lines of option 3. That is, the church determined that "the principal responsibility for systematic Christian education lies with the church," but added that "provision will be made for an educational ministry to families" which would offer parents "guidance both in understanding themselves and their children and in discovering how to speak to their children's questions and concerns."[18]

At the present time, there seems to be no particular policy in many denominations. This has been the case, at least, in most churches involved in the *Christian Education: Shared Approaches* effort of Joint Educational Development. Instead, we have multiple practices in various congregations which include a continuation of option 3 and experiments in many of the rest of the options.

Some congregations are experimenting with intergenerational education, while others are trying "family cluster" education and marriage and/or family enrichment. Both are examples of option 2. Many congregations provide courses for various family members (adult, youth, or children) on such topics as human sexuality, marriage preparation, parenting, understanding parents, dealing with family conflicts, coping with economic difficulties, divorce, and others. These are all examples of option 3. Still other congregations are providing courses and workshops that teach parents both to live out their Christian vocation as parents in new ways *and* to engage in the Christian education of their children in the home as a part of this vocation. The work that James and Kathleen McGinnis are doing in the Parenting for Peace and Justice program comes to mind and provides an example of option 6. A practice once rather prominent but now fallen into disuse brought the pastor into homes to "catechize" the whole family unit (an example of option 1). This is a practice that was and would be inadequate in isolation from other approaches, but it might provide some clues for new practices of education which in another way take family homes more seriously as contexts for education.

These ways of thinking about education in relation to church and family are not mutually exclusive; indeed, they in some ways overlap and can usefully complement and strengthen one another. What is important to see is the variety of possibilities. This keeps us from thinking that "family education" is just one thing, and fosters creativity. When we think about families and Christian education, we must not limit ourselves to thinking in terms of "family" as only the subject matter of education in relationship to families. The family and family issues can and should be part of *what* we teach and learn about in Christian education, but we must also think of families as *who* learns and teaches. Families can be teachers and learners *as families* (both in clusters and alone). And the family dwelling can be a setting for Christian education, as a place *where* Christian education takes place. In relation to Christian education, "family"

means neither *just* subject matter, nor just participants, nor
just setting, but all of these in various combinations.

What we do in Christian education in relation to family,
and how we do it, must be decided on the basis of what we
hope for. There are, to my mind, three hopes or aims that are
particularly significant at the nexus of faith and family. The
first of these is that all Christian family members become
aware of, understand, and affirm their promises to each
other and come to see these in the context of the broader
covenants they make as Christians. The second is that they
increasingly learn the skills appropriate to and required for
redemptive life in the context of family relationships. And
the third is that they learn to be family as a distinctive
partnership in their activity of faith in the world.

Each of these aims is slightly different, and the educational approaches that we use will have to be varied in order
to work toward them all. The first aim places a stress on
awareness and understanding as preludes to affirmation.
This requires both information and reflection. Here courses
on the theology of the family, biblical and theological study
of the promises and covenants involved in Christian faith as
a whole, and on our covenantal liturgies (especially marriage and Baptism) would be important. Such courses would
need to present the church's history and thought on these
matters and provide opportunities for people to reflect on
them and on their own family lives in relation to them. They
might best be done differently for different family members
in ways appropriate to their ages, levels of reflective ability,
and situations. In connection with such courses, however, we
should also find ways to help family members to talk to each
other about what they have discovered and whatever affirmations they make of family promises to them and to each
other. Such courses then would be especially important as
part of preparation for making promises in marriage, baptismal, confirmation, or ordination and/or installation liturgies. They could also help people think through what happens to their promises in such situations as children leaving

the home (perhaps to begin new families), divorce, or the death of a family member. From another perspective, they might also serve to help the church think through the question of whether other liturgies might also be developed and used to lift up and secure family promises—and then be used to help the people to understand and participate fully in such liturgies if they were adopted. Some examples might be liturgies for *(a)* blessing infants who are not to be baptized until adulthood and charging the parent or parents and the congregation with their care and nurture; *(b)* blessing and charging members of the congregation who are moving away; and *(c)* blessing homes when families move into them.

The second aim focuses on the development of skills, and this involves practice. Action/reflection educational strategies in contexts that make them possible are crucial here. Learning such skills as communicating effectively, dealing with conflict, sharing material goods and possessions, praying, worshiping, working for peace and justice, becoming conscious of and resisting subtle forms of violence and manipulation require more than presentation and reflection. They require the development of new habits through thoughtful engagement in action (practice) until new ways of living seem more natural. Sometimes this can occur in church buildings, but often other settings must be found. Certainly, we must find ways to help each other eventually "practice" these skills in our homes. For this sort of education, options 5, 7, and 8 will not do.

The third aim—that families learn to be family as a distinctive partnership in the activity of faith—is not so much a separate aim as what the other two (and the educational approaches that foster them) would, we hope, lead to. But stating this aim separately helps us to see that an educational practice that does not involve *both* congregational responsibility and family responsibility, education in both church and home, will not be adequate. There can be no doubt about how difficult this is and about what a high degree of responsibility it places on family members (especially parents) and on educational leaders in congregations and the various agencies of the church. If we were to think and work along these lines, we would have to be willing to encounter a good deal of frustration, failure, and disappointment. But that is in the nature of educational ministry. Often we never see many of the results of such ministry. The results that we do see often seem minimal, and always fall far short of what we hope for. But that is not the point. The point is simply to be faithful to the promises of God to us and to the promises we make in return.

Families are changing in many ways. They are not, and never have been, perfect. That is true also, of course, of congregations—indeed, of the whole church in all its forms of partnership. But the promises of God hold forever. They are promises to us as a church, as congregations, as families, and as individuals, calling us to respond with promises of our own. We cannot, we would not, live on any other terms.

7

Family Ministries and the Local Church

Carol Rose Ikeler

The liveliest discussions among parents attending family ministries workshops that I have conducted revolve around issues such as spanking, marriage enrichment, the family and Christian feminism, and homosexuality. Let's begin with a sampling from some of these discussions.

Spanking. This issue surfaces in a workshop segment on preventing family violence. The consensus that finally emerges tends to be: Any form of hitting is wrong, and parent support groups and training in parenting skills and conflict management are critically needed. Caring parents learn to ask themselves: What do children learn from spanking? Simply, not to do it again? What key message are they getting about love and morality? That it's okay for people who love each other to hit each other?

Marriage enrichment. Questions arise as to why marriage counseling is an important responsibility for the church. There is generally consensus that communication skills are essential for husbands and wives, as couples and as parents in a family setting. It is also noted that there are many stable *single-parent* families in the 1980s, and that support groups are greatly needed for family health and stability in both settings. There is also recognition that only churches can supply the essential biblical, theological, and spiritual dimensions that Christian homes need.

The family and Christian feminism. Workshop groups have reflected on a recent book by Letty Pogrebin, titled *Family Politics,* [1] in which there is a compelling defense of the sometimes beleaguered institution of the family by one who is a parent and a feminist. Pogrebin argues that family and gender equality need not be in conflict, and that there is a new kind of democratic family in the 1980s that is energized by reciprocity and partnership rather than by hierarchy, domination, or excessive permissiveness. Perhaps most important of all, groups, sparked by Pogrebin's insights, are able to explore the distinctiveness of Reformed biblical theology regarding the family as emphasized in contemporary confessions of the church, [2] and surmount the confusion created by biblical literalism and the resulting conflict in male-female relationships and family authority.

Homosexuality. Responses range from embarrassment, biblical confusion, and profound concern to tearful parental confessions. The pivotal question raised is: Are churches really open and caring enough to help in this kind of family anguish?

What do Christians do about such issues—the gut reality of people's lives? How can a local church be responsible in helping families experience the wholeness that is clearly the gospel's intent? A two-part answer emerges repeatedly in the many workshops offered by the Presbyterian Office of Family Ministries (Atlanta) in partnership with presbyteries, synods, and women's groups. What we have learned may parallel the insights of other church bodies as they too look for answers to the issues of family life.

1. Congregations and church boards need to engage in detailed thinking about what ministry to families really is and how it can be carried out. Then they must act upon the concepts they have developed and undertake implementation even if only in modest beginnings.

2. We must find the resources and skills needed for the planning and action indicated in the above paragraph. In the words of a contemporary confession, "The church comes under the judgment of God and invites rejection by society

when it fails to lead men and women into the full meaning of life together, or withholds the compassion of Christ from those caught in the moral confusion of our time."[3]

FAMILY MINISTRY IN A NEW KEY

Throughout the twentieth century, Protestant denominations have been engaged in various forms of ministry to families, at the national and local levels. Craig Dykstra reminds us of various important past experiments in Presbyterian resources for church and home. But the 1980s is a time of unprecedented change for families; the challenge for the church is even greater today than it was in previous decades. Consequently, we are now hearing new messages, such as those expressed in the Ghost Ranch Symposium, and we are hearing with new ears what the Spirit is saying to us through the Scriptures and documents of the church.

There is much public debate today concerning the state of the family. There is also considerable handwringing on the part of some Christians. Many others, however, while recognizing the numerous problems that confront the family in these turbulent times, nevertheless view perceptual alarm and fits of nostalgia as inappropriate responses. They perceive with scholars such as James Nelson, author of the landmark study on sexuality, *Embodiment,* that present-day change in the family is no novelty, because in fact the family has always been changing.[4]

We can all agree that in this era when traditional family structures are in disarray, the need to reflect, identify issues, plan more systematically, and act in new ways has become more urgent for local churches that seek to be faithful in ministry. Because of the exciting work of family researchers such as Hamilton and Marilyn McCubbin, there is increasing discussion as to what constitutes genuine family ministries in the name of Jesus Christ. More and more churches are striving for a broader and more inclusive understanding of what constitutes family in the 1980s. Many are recognizing the need for a clear profile of the size and "shape" of each member family; officers and staff are maintaining up-to-date card files and charts to document family style. In addition, there is a serious process of assessment of the interests and needs of *families* in the church, as well as of individuals, peers, and sexes. Some churches, for example, mail out questionnaires, or insert them in the Sunday order of worship, and then collect and dedicate them at offering time. Today, more congregations are seeking to provide opportunities to enhance the strengths and well-being of families, while continuing to provide the usual basic services of counseling for brokenness and crises.

As a result, family ministry is becoming increasingly intentional at the local church level; that is to say, it is being carried out with disciplined strategy and coordinated planning by governing boards and committees. Family ministry may be led by a chairperson who is a member of a Christian education committee, or by someone who heads up a special task force on the family. No longer is family life program an occasional thing, such as an Advent potluck or a Lenten film. Along with worship and stewardship, family ministry is increasingly seen as a pervasive concept, a primary concern that is basic to the total nurture of the congregation, whatever the size of its membership. Indeed, some imaginative leaders are now seeing family ministry as a holistic way of "thinking" and ordering the entire household of faith. The emphasis is on ministry to, with, and by *family units* as well as individuals.

Moreover, Christians are becoming aware of the powerful reality of "family systems," a fairly recent contribution to our thinking from the behavioral sciences. This concept focuses on the perception that all the values and actions of a family impact on each individual member and vice versa. The family is a "system" of interrelated persons and feelings. (Hence the current emphasis in psychology on *family*/group counseling—that is, one person's difficulty cannot be dealt with independent of the family community.) Obviously, the implications of this outlook for the local church are highly significant.[5]

In the reemergence in new forms for the 1980s of what used to be called "family life education," the church stands to gain from the findings of family researchers such as the McCubbins, who reinforce our theological understanding that

> families appear to benefit from social contacts they develop within programs, and in direct contact with people, church affiliations, and friendships within the community. This type of support through natural groups and human contacts has healing quality in protecting families from adversity and in facilitating their adaptation following a major crisis. Families appear to benefit from emotional support, esteem support, network support, appraisal support, and altruistic support. In other words, families are placing a greater emphasis upon social and human contacts to get the basic nurturance and understanding which is essential in managing stressful life events.[6]

If we really believe the Bible's message that the church exists *for the sake of the world,* and that its task is "to equip the saints for the work of ministry, for building up the body of Christ" (Eph. 4:12), then there are at least two essential facets to an intentional ongoing program of support and empowerment of families. The first is an orchestrated cycle of engaging families of the church in theologically oriented marriage enrichment and parenting support/skill groups that are strengthening and empowering, rather than crisis oriented and remedial. This is not to say that churches can in the least relax their ministries to persons in crisis situations. On the contrary, situations of family violence, divorce, death of spouse, or chronic illness must be responded to.

Parallel and closely related is a second facet, that of the enabling of families as well as of individuals, to minister with and to families elsewhere in the community and the world, through awareness and skills related to local and global issues. Here we are concretely and movingly instructed by the McGinnises' model of "parenting for peace and justice."[7] Families as well as individuals are called to be

Christ's agents of healing and wholeness, his ambassadors for Christian evangelism.

PLANNING FOR FAMILY MINISTRIES IN A NEW KEY

An example of the new efforts on the part of American Christians to take seriously and respond to the needs of families in the 1980s and 1990s is the Ghost Ranch Symposium and the publication of its papers. This venture was a collaborative one in which Atlanta and New York family staff perceived a need and responded to it. In the not too distant future we will continue this work nationally as one staff and one office.

Our work is in partnership with presbyteries, synods, women's groups, conference centers, leaders of other church bodies, and councils of churches. Activities involve workshop models that include resources for local church programs, discussions of public issues, and areas of family ministry such as marriage enrichment, parenting skills, sexuality, aging, family violence, the handicapped, racial/ethnic families, life-style, and planning/doing. Workshop components may include annotated bibliographies such as the *Family Ministry Resource and Program Guide,* videocassette, film, and filmstrip resources, packets of literature, and items such as *A Guide to Parenting Programs: An Appraisal of Seven Major Parenting Programs.* [8]

If we are to be effective agents for encouraging families to grow in faith, pastors, church officers, and other leaders will need resources and skills in planning and doing family ministries. One of the most useful resources in leadership training and facilitating is Joe Leonard's slender but valuable paperback, *Planning Family Ministry.* [9] In the six brief chapters, creative guidance is provided regarding tasks (educational, theological, advocacy), content and skill areas, biblical foundations, today's changing families, steps to planning, and a comprehensive ministry to families. Authors such as

Leonard do a great service to the church in providing reliable insight, from both the social sciences and religious studies, for developing family ministries in a new key.

BIBLICAL HERMENEUTICS IN A NEW KEY

As God's word has been spoken in diverse cultural situations, the church is confident that God will continue to speak through the Scriptures in a changing world and in every form of human culture.[10]

When we encounter apparent tensions and conflicts
    in what Scripture teaches us to believe and do,
        the final appeal must be to the authority of Christ.
Acknowledging that authority,
    comparing Scripture with Scripture,
    listening with respect to fellow-believers past and present,
        we anticipate that the Holy Spirit
        will enable us to interpret faithfully
God's Word for our time and place.[11]

In family ministry workshops we often hear the cry, "If people would just get back to the Bible, the family wouldn't be in such a mess!" One's immediate internal response has to be, "What really lies behind that statement?" After pondering Judith Kovacs' exciting and informative chapter "Faith and Family in Biblical Perspective" in this collection, one fervently wishes that a gift copy of her essay could be shared with each questioner.

The hermeneutic (ways or theories of interpretation) is highly important, as Kovacs points out, in relating the Bible and family relationships. We have tried to respond constructively to this yearning to apply the Bible's insight to family life by publishing *A Guide to Parenting Programs.* This resource examines seven major parenting programs currently in use in churches in terms of how "family" is defined, the approach to biblical interpretation and authority issues, and a number of other indices. Excerpts from

Presbyterian confessional documents that pertain to the use of the Bible are included in the *Guide* for the benefit of the local church planner as he or she seeks to evaluate various family resources. Though it is keyed to churches in the Reformed tradition, church bodies in other traditions could adapt it for use in relation to their own planning for parent education.

When we hear that cry of perplexity, "If the family would just get back to the Bible . . . ," we try to share the insights of biblical scholars such as Judith Kovacs. They point to the rich diversity of the Bible regarding the family, including the early patriarchal models with many wives, concubines, and slaves, and the house-church families like Timothy's with Grandmother Lois and Mother Eunice (2 Tim. 1:5). But most especially they point us to an interpretive approach that focuses on the ministry, message, and meaning of Christ. Such an approach is characterized by emphasis on equality, mutuality and liberation in the New Age.

An illustration of family and biblical interpretation from the perspective of liberation theology and ethics is found in the work of Francis E. Ringer in a paper prepared as background study for United Church of Christ leaders planning strategy for that denomination's emphasis on family. I should like to review his paper here.[12] Ringer represents important insights that reflect the impact of Third World, black, Hispanic, Asian, and feminist Christians on theological thought in the past two decades. These new voices are concerned with the personal experience of widespread discrimination and economic oppression in the twentieth century. Their understanding of Jesus is shaped by their condition of oppression; in his own life and experience they see a reflection of their own, and in his message and work the path and power of liberation.

Ringer reminds us that theology is a human enterprise—that even with revelation, "our knowledge of God is still 'managed' within human experience." He then leads us to his own hermeneutic, his biblical approach to understanding the family in the 1980s. He writes:

A helpful book premised upon this human experience perspective is *Christology at the Crossroads,* by Jon Sobrino (Orbis Books, 1978), which is probably to date the only fine attempt at Christology from the liberation viewpoint. He attempts to explore Christology "from the bottom up," in liberation language. The key to his endeavor is the rejection of prior concepts of God as a means of explaining the phenomenon of Jesus. Instead, he explores the life of Jesus as experienced by his disciples, striving to discover the insights into God which they gained as they lived with Jesus. By a careful study of the records of the New Testament, Sobrino also attempts to surmise some of the changing views of God in the experience of Jesus himself. In all that happened in the life of Jesus and in the lives of those who were his closest companions arose new insights into God. The disciples experienced the unique phenomenon of Jesus of Nazareth, and from this experience they came to unique insights within their human understanding of the nature of God. We continue to succumb often to doing theology from the top down, approaching it with all manner of preconceptions about what God "must" be like, and generally the preconceptions are more Greek than Hebrew, more rooted in speculative philosophy than in an interpretation of human experience in living. To do Christology, suggests Sobrino, we must start with the reality of Jesus and attempt to grasp what the disciples surmised about God through their life experience with Jesus. Next we explore the experiences of subsequent followers, who built upon the experiences they had with their mentors, until we come to our own experiences within the Christian community of believers. The perspective remains, however, that of asking what we grasp of God within our own life context and through the life experiences of those who believe and attempt to walk in Christ.

After that important illustration for understanding the hermeneutic and methodology of liberation theology, Ringer offers some stimulating thoughts on "doing" a theology of the family. He writes:

The structure of the family in our time has been undergoing change, and as Christians study this phenomenon they find themselves immediately in the tension noted by Sobrino. Do we study the family from prior conceptions or do we study the family from within the dynamic realities of present human interrelations? Do we begin with abstractions rooted in concepts of God and of some law of society, attempting then to bring human relationships into conformity with this top-down ideal? Or do we begin with an investigation into the dynamics of human relationships as they exist now and endeavor to learn from them something about God and the ways of the people of God in this moment in human history? This would be akin to Sobrino's thesis that the disciples learned about God through Jesus more than they understood Jesus through their preconceptions about God. Do some of us now claim to know too much about God's plans for families and now understand too little about God's gracious ways with humans already engaged in variations of human relationships? Do we simply refuse to consider some of the new relationships as even possible avenues through which we may learn something about God, by God's grace? Shall we impose a fixed form upon a dynamic relationship among humans, as many suggest? Shall we abandon all guiding principles in human relationships? Or shall we seek a fitting response to both questions, a response lying between the extremes most likely?

Ringer continues with some penetrating questions about the nuclear family, which he and others remind us emerged in the industrial revolution and is now struggling under the pressure of what Alvin Toffler calls the "Third Wave," an era of technology marked by electronics.[13]

Do we freeze the family here [in the Second Wave, the industrial age]? Ironically, do we call upon structures of the agrarian age to reinforce our commitment to the family of the industrial age, pleading the Old Testament to defend our Second Wave nuclear family?

Ringer then describes the many family configurations in our present Third Wave of civilization: the blended, the single-parented, and others, such as Sawyers, Lowry, and others have considered. He asks a penetrating theological question: "What do we do with such realities in our world today? Do we mold these to preconceptions [of an earlier age] or do we strive somehow to perceive God at work in and through these dynamic human relationships?"

He then mentions the important distinction that Sobrino makes between *following* Christ as disciples and *imitating* Jesus of Nazareth.

> To imitate is to attempt to freeze life as it was, or was thought to be, in some past time. To follow as a disciple, suggests Sobrino, is to move forward through various cultural configurations over the ages, including the daring reformulations of our own time. . . . Endeavoring to be obedient to the Christ moving onward, the church has been imaginative in its faithfulness as it has sought to follow Christ around surprising corners and strange turns. To follow is to go forth in faith, centering upon dynamic relationships rather than upon preconceived forms rooted in a static past or absolute abstraction. . . . As Christians we believe this world is God's and we are a form of counter-culture. We would do well to try to understand God from the realities of the world in which God has called us into life as the church, attempting to discover God by reading the experience of this world from the bottom up. As we discern the "signs of the times" in our reading of experience we as Christians also use the Bible as a source of guidance but not always of prescriptions. We seek to be followers more than imitators.

Ringer is suggesting that we who are concerned about the family might ask a question of hope rather than joining the handwringers over the "demise of the family" or those who look back in the Scriptures for old models. The question might be phrased, "What is God saying to us through the new and different configurations of family in the 1980s?"

Ringer's provocative insights for ethics and biblical theology of the family tie in with some of Judith Kovacs' major conclusions:

> The biblical word for families is not contained solely, or even primarily, in the specific commandments about family life but rather in the central proclamations of the Bible. We can infer this from the way the Bible uses family images and stories. The central question for Christian families is not "What are the biblical laws, or even the biblical models, for us?" but "How are we to live out our theology—the central affirmations of our faith—in the intimate spheres of our lives together?"[14]

"FAMILYING" FOR PEACE AND JUSTICE

In the crucial realms of love and justice the local church that cares has had a "big assist" in getting it all together—namely, the book, program, and movement called Parenting for Peace and Justice (PPJ). Throughout mainline Protestantism as well as their own Roman Catholic constituency, James and Kathleen McGinnis continue to be a profound blessing as they share themselves unstintingly to further the cause of shalom in family, community, and the world. They model not only the basic ingredients of their theology—a faith journey rooted in the New Testament gospel of love and justice, mature married love, and learned parenting skills (such as regular and genuine family meeting decision-making)—but also a sincere and contagious ecumenism that can unite the most diverse gatherings.

In a recent family ministry workshop that included a discussion of the PPJ programs, an older woman was objecting to the concern for role stereotyping, "a legacy of the women's lib that messes up the family," as she described it. Very quickly a young man noted that only during that past week it was reported in the news media that the women of Switzerland had won the right to have personal bank accounts and checkbooks and to know how much income the family could expect. "All that Victorian patriarchal injustice in one of the most advanced technologically pioneering countries in the Western world!" he said, then added, "Thank God for programs like PPJ."

One could wish that in their chapter, the McGinnises had included more about the controversial area of education for sexuality—so important for church families, theologically and spiritually. The McGinnises do deal indirectly with an important aspect of this subject in what they say about the family's monitoring of television commercials and programs for violence and gender stereotyping.

Many family ministry leaders are suggesting as support material in sexuality another reliable resource, the five video lectures, *Creating Family,* for adults and teens, by a Roman Catholic psychiatrist, Clayton Barbeau. There is also a variety of reliable denominational publications for various age groups on sexuality and married love.[15] James Nelson's book *Embodiment* continues to be one of the most substantial resources for faithful leadership by the church in a sexually troubled society.

One important area in family ministries that does not receive direct attention in PPJ or in this symposium, except for a brief mention by Hamilton and Marilyn McCubbin, is the family with a handicapped member. The Presbyterian Church has made some conscientious efforts in ministry with disabled persons and their families during the last two decades. (Among these efforts is the publication of *Special Edition,* a newsletter published by the Presbyterian Program Agency in New York.) Nonetheless, the number of inaccessible churches remains unacceptably large. Here, surely, is an urgent family justice issue for every congregation. Again, the initiating of cluster or ecumenical support groups for family care givers is tremendously needed, not in order to compete with such groups under secular auspices but because of the critical theological dimension without which wholeness cannot be experienced.

With these and similar issues in mind, the Office of Family Ministries (Atlanta) facilitated a workshop for parents of disabled children as part of the annual Family Enrichment Conferences at the Montreat Conference Center, North Carolina, and made funds available for registration scholarships. Five families with handicapped children participated.

An additional area of pressing concern is ministry with the elderly, the importance of which is underlined in Janet Huber Lowry's chapter. With Lowry's statistics about the swift "aging of America," and the creative program and network of the Presbyterian Office of Aging (Atlanta and New York), Presbyterians have a clear call to comprehend and act. (An excellent filmstrip, *Up Golden Creek*—with a

Spanish edition as well as an English edition—continues to be an important tool for family ministry programming.)

Finally, those concerned with ministry to the increasing number of nontraditional families welcome the developing body of literature on the liberation of men. In the *Family Ministry Resource and Program Guide,* mentioned above, many books are listed that deal with changing, flexible roles of men and women. A small new paperback from Augsburg Press carries a message on the cover, important to parenting for peace and justice and to family ministries in a new key:

> There is hope for men! It *is* possible to be masculine without always being tough, aggressive, and unemotional. You *can* change, adapt, and discover new ways of relating—and in the process become a better husband, father, and friend. *New Life for Men* brings together the best of psychology and the Bible to provide you with practical help to develop new attitudes, roles, and behavior. It gives you courage and confidence to grow, change, and begin a new male journey.[16]

In a wonderfully provocative book for parents, *Is God the Only Reliable Father?*[17] Diane Tennis urges Christians not to abandon the father image of God. She also focuses upon the contemporary situation of the family and the biblical understanding of God who transcends patriarchal models. She presents as an example for contemporary males the Jesus who truly affirms women. Her understanding of male/female and the family in the 1980s is challenging for both families and faith.

In the past decade the church has gradually begun to take seriously the liberation of men from the stultifying, traditional macho roles. A new literature is emerging in which men who sense the importance of the ongoing contribution of Christian feminism are beginning to ask important questions about their humanity in the light of social science and to inquire what it means to be male and female "in Christ." See, for example, James Dittes' *The Male Predicament.*[18]

POSTSCRIPT

In fulfilling my task of providing the concluding chapter in this symposium, I have had two special commitments.

First, I have tried throughout to begin with my own experience of issues affecting real families and churches in the 1980s, rather than with theological doctrines or first principles. The latter, of course, I do not reject, as is evident in the segments quoted from Presbyterian confessions. Moreover, I have included salient excerpts from contemporary biblical theologians who can be our "tutors unto Christ" on family themes in a *new key.*

Second, I have read and reread the symposium contributors, reflected upon them for many weeks, then sought to interpret and supplement them regarding family ministries in my capacity as a full-time minister, past and present, to all kinds of Presbyterian families.

As I listen to our writers, it seems to me that this book is a genuine breakthrough; I receive from them orders for the future in the spirit of *New* Testament theology. I hear them saying in various ways and to varying degrees that for faith and families there is no returning to earlier notions of family life; that authority and sexuality, two basic ingredients of family life, are rooted in the equality, mutuality, and liberation of Jesus Christ—his personal relationships, his message, his resurrection, and the experience of his followers.

With their own special expertise, the symposium contributors have pointed to areas and issues to which churches must give careful thought.

Kovacs: A new provocative *biblical hermeneutic* that characterizes religious ecumenical studies in the 1980s, lifting up the liberation of male and female as a challenge for families rooted in the Bible.

Lowry: Mind-boggling demographics that remind us that our ministry must be grounded in a profound sense of the new configurations embraced by the word "family"—the single parent, the aging, the blended, and all the rest.

McCubbin: New, exciting findings of the social sciences from *research with real families,* with tremendous implications for family ministries.

McGinnis: Powerful critique of the destructive values of our society that oppress *all* families, growing out of the gods of an exploitative competitive economic order; the urgency for the church to help families be a part of *Christ's resisting alternative* which the Bible mandates. Understanding and doing shalom is the key.

Lee: A heightened view of the sphere of the family as a setting to glorify God, and a deepened concern for the pain of dislocation and adjustment in *intercultural and racial/ethnic* families in the 1980s.

Dykstra: A new look at the importance of *making and living our promises* in the 1980s as part of genuine Christian existence.

The work of the Symposium on "Faith and Families" must now continue, in our lives, in our congregations and their governing boards, and in our denominations. The time has come to move from thought to action—from knowing to faithful response.

Notes

1. FAITH AND FAMILY IN BIBLICAL PERSPECTIVE / KOVACS

1. For a discussion of different types of family, see Charles R. Taber, "Kinship and Family," *The Interpreter's Dictionary of the Bible, Supplementary Volume* (Abingdon Press, 1976), pp. 519–524.

2. Otto J. Baab, "Family," *The Interpreter's Dictionary of the Bible,* Vol. 2 (Abingdon Press, 1962), p. 238.

3. For a detailed description of social structure in ancient Israel, see Norman K. Gottwald, *The Tribes of Yahweh: A Sociology of the Religion of Liberated Israel 1250–1050* B.C.E. (Orbis Books, 1979), pp. 237–341. Gottwald attempts to define precisely the various senses of terms such as "family," "clan," and "tribe." Note Gottwald's subtitle, which limits his treatment to a particular period in Israel's history. Generalizations about "the biblical family" such as those I have made here should not be taken to mean that there were no changes in family structure during the more than two thousand years of history reflected in the Bible.

4. Robert Hamerton-Kelly, in *God the Father: Theology and Patriarchy in the Teaching of Jesus* (Fortress Press, 1979), p. 20, lists eleven texts in which God is designated as "father" as well as several other texts where God's "parenthood" is implied.

5. See Hamerton-Kelly, *God the Father,* pp. 52ff.

6. Translation by Hamerton-Kelly, *God the Father,* p. 39. He argues that the mother image, not the father image, is predominant in Hosea 11.

7. Krister Stendahl, *The Bible and the Role of Women: A Case Study in Hermeneutics* (Fortress Press, 1966), p. 40. Compare p. 17: "It is highly doubtful that God wants us to play First-Century Semite."

8. Ernst Käsemann, *New Testament Questions of Today* (Fortress Press, 1969), "Worship in Everyday Life: A Note on Romans 12," pp. 188–195.

9. Masamba Ma Mpolo, ed., *Family Profiles* (Geneva: World Council of Churches, 1984); Kathleen and James McGinnis, *Parenting for Peace and Justice* (Orbis Books, 1981).

10. On this point, compare the chapter by Sang H. Lee in this volume.

11. Cf. Joseph A. Fitzmyer, S.J., *The Gospel According to Luke (X–XXIV),* Anchor Bible (Doubleday & Co., 1985), p. 1063.

12. Compare Jesus' rebuff of his mother and brothers in Mark 3:33–35 and the call of the disciples in Mark 1:20, which may echo the call of Abraham—"and Abram went"—(Gen. 12:4). Compare also the sayings in Mark 10:29; Matt. 19:21; Luke 8:19–21 and the chapter by Sang H. Lee in this volume.

13. For an extreme statement of this view, see Mary Daly, *Beyond God the Father: Toward a Philosophy of Women's Liberation* (Beacon Press, 1973).

14. Elisabeth Schüssler Fiorenza, *In Memory of Her: A Feminist Theological Reconstruction of Christian Origins* (Crossroad Publishing Co., 1984); for a summary of feminist biblical scholarship, see pp. 3–40. See also Phyllis Trible, *God and the Rhetoric of Sexuality* (Fortress Press, 1978); Phyllis Trible, *Texts of Terror: Literary-Feminist Readings of Biblical Narratives* (Fortress Press, 1984); and Hamerton-Kelly, *God the Father.*

15. Robin Scroggs, "Paul and the Eschatological Woman," *JAAR,* Vol. 40 (1972), p. 283.

16. For this and other statements in this chapter about the general conclusions of historical-critical study of the New Testament, see a standard introduction—for example, Norman Perrin and Dennis C. Duling, *The New Testament: An Introduction,* 2d ed. (Harcourt Brace Jovanovich, 1982).

17. For a survey of the extensive secondary literature on Paul's view of women, see Schüssler Fiorenza, *In Memory of Her,* pp. 205–241.

18. On Paul's interpretation of the death of Jesus, cf. J. Christiaan Beker, *Paul the Apostle: The Triumph of God in Life and Thought* (Fortress Press, 1980), pp. 182–212.

19. In addition to the works by Daly, Schüssler Fiorenza, and Trible cited in notes 13 and 14, see Elizabeth A. Clark, *Women in the Early Church* (Wilmington, Del.: Michael Glazier, 1983), for the interpretation of biblical texts by the church fathers.

20. Hamerton-Kelly, *God the Father,* pp. 69–70.

21. Robert Bellah, "Walk Away . . . Don't Look Back: Rampant Individualism," *Concern,* Winter 1985, pp. 18–19.

22. See Schüssler Fiorenza, *In Memory of Her,* pp. 343–351.

2. FAMILIES IN CHURCH AND SOCIETY / LOWRY

1. Paul C. Glick, "American Household Structure in Transition," *Family Planning Perspectives,* Vol. 16, No. 5 (September/October 1984), p. 210.

2. Andrew J. Cherlin, *Marriage, Divorce, Remarriage* (Harvard University Press, 1981), pp. 13–14.

3. Glick, "American Household Structure in Transition."

4. Arland Thornton and Deborah Freedman, "The Changing American Family," *Population Bulletin,* Vol. 38, No. 4 (October 1983), p. 10.

5. Cherlin, *Marriage, Divorce, Remarriage,* p. 30.

6. Glick, "American Household Structure in Transition," p. 211.

7. Theodore D. Kemper, "Predicting the Divorce Rate—Down?" *Journal of Family Issues,* Vol. 4, No. 3 (September 1983), pp. 507–524.

8. Thorton and Freedman, "The Changing American Family," p. 8.

9. Glick, "American Household Structure in Transition," p. 211.

10. Sandra L. Hofferth, "Updating Children's Life Course," *Journal of Marriage and the Family,* Vol. 47, No. 1 (February 1985), pp. 93–115.

11. Judith Senderowitz and John M. Paxman, "Adolescent Fertility: Worldwide Concerns," *Population Bulletin,* Vol. 40, No. 2 (April 1985), p. 15.

12. Ibid., p. 26.

13. "Child Poverty Levels Soaring," in the *Sherman Democrat Thursday,* May 23, 1985, from AP newswire.

14. Carol Tavris and Carole Wade, *The Longest War: Sex Differences in Perspective,* 2d ed. (Harcourt Brace Jovanovich, 1984), p. 286.

15. William P. Butz and others, *Demographic Challenges in America's Future* (Rand Corporation, 1982).

16. Wendy H. Baldwin and Christine Winquist Nord, "Delayed Childbearing in the U.S.: Facts and Fictions," *Population Bulletin,* Vol. 39, No. 4 (November 1984).

17. Kerry Richter, "Nonmetropolitan Growth in the late 1970s: The End of the Turnaround?" *Demography*, Vol. 22, No. 2 (May 1985), pp. 245–264.

18. William H. Frey, "Move Destination Selectivity and the Changing Suburbanization of Metropolitan Whites and Blacks," *Demography*, Vol. 22, No. 2 (May 1985), pp. 223–244.

19. Barry Bluestone and Bennett Harrison, "Boomtown and Busttown," in *Crisis in American Institutions*, ed. Jerome H. Skolnick and Elliott Currie, 6th ed. (Little, Brown & Co., 1985).

20. "The State of Families 1984–85," Family Service America, 1984.

21. Population Reference Bureau staff and guest experts, "U.S. Population: Where Are We; Where Are We Going?" *Population Bulletin*, Vol. 37, No. 2 (June 1982).

22. *Publication Needs of the Presbyterian Church, U.S.A. Appendix I. Summary of The American Presbyterian* (New York: Research Unit, Support Agency, Presbyterian Church (U.S.A.), 1984).

23. *The Presbyterians: A Background Report on Those Who Constitute the Panel and on the Reestablishment of the Panel* (New York: Research Unit, Support Agency, United Presbyterian Church U.S.A., 1982), pp. 9f.

24. Ibid., p. 10.

25. Hofferth, "Updating Children's Life Course."

26. Cherlin, *Marriage, Divorce, Remarriage.*

3. RESILIENT FAMILIES, COMPETENCIES,
SUPPORTS, AND COPING
McCUBBIN AND McCUBBIN

1. C. Vincent, "Familia Spongia: The Adaptive Function," *Journal of Marriage and the Family*, Vol. 28, No. 1 (Feb., 1966), pp. 29–36.

2. H. McCubbin and J. Patterson, "Family Transitions: Adaptation to Stress," in *Stress and the Family, Volume I: Coping with Normative Transitions*, ed. Hamilton I. McCubbin and Charles R. Figley (Brunner/Mazel, 1983); and H. McCubbin and J. Patterson, "The Family Stress Process: The Double ABCX Model of Adjustment and Adaptation," in *Social Stress and the Family: Advances and Developments in Family Stress Theory and Research*, ed. Hamilton I. McCubbin, Marvin B. Sussman, and Joan M. Patterson (Haworth Press, 1983).

3. René Dubos, *So Human an Animal* (Charles Scribner's Sons, 1968).

4. *Native Hawaiian Education Assessment Project* (Honolulu, Hawaii: Kamehameha Schools and Bishop Estate, 1983).

5. H. McCubbin, D. H. Olson, and S. Zimmerman, "Family Action Research: Stress, Strengths, Therapy, and Policy," in *Action Research in Social Sciences,* ed. R. Rappoport (Guilford Press.) (In press.)

6. H. McCubbin and others, "The Returned Prisoner of War: Factors in Family Reintegration," *Journal of Marriage and the Family,* Vol. 37, No. 3 (Aug., 1975), pp. 471–478.

7. Aaron Antonovsky, *Health, Stress, and Coping* (Jossey-Bass, 1979).

8. H. McCubbin and others, "Developing Family Invulnerability to Stress: Coping Patterns and Strategies Wives Employ in Managing Family Separations," in *The Family in Change,* ed. J. Trost (Västers, Sweden: International Library, 1980); H. McCubbin and J. Patterson, "Broadening the Scope of Family Strengths: An Emphasis on Family Coping and Social Support," in *Family Strengths 3: Roots of Well-Being,* ed. Nick Stinnett and others (University of Nebraska Press, 1981); and J. Patterson and H. McCubbin, "Chronic Illnesses: Family Stress and Coping," in *Stress and the Family,* Volume II: *Coping with Catastrophe,* ed. Charles R. Figley and Hamilton I. McCubbin (Brunner/Mazel, 1983).

9. J. Patterson and H. McCubbin, "Gender Roles and Coping," *Journal of Marriage and the Family,* Vol. 46, No. 1 (Feb., 1984), pp. 145–455.

10. M. McCubbin, "Nursing Assessment of Parental Coping with Cystic Fibrosis," *Western Journal of Nursing Research,* Vol. 6, No. 4 (Fall, 1984), pp. 407–422; J. Comeau, "Family Resources in the Care of the Chronically Ill Child" (unpublished doctoral dissertation, University of Minnesota, Dissertation Abstracts, University of Michigan); and Patterson and McCubbin (1983), "Gender Roles and Coping."

11. David H. Olson and others, *Families: What Makes Them Work* (Sage Publications, 1983).

12. Hamilton I. McCubbin, J. Patterson, and Y. Lavee, *One Thousand Army Families: Stress, Coping, and Supports* (University of Minnesota, 1985).

13. David R. Mace, *Getting Ready for Marriage* (Abingdon Press, 1972); and David R. Mace, "Marriage Enrichment: The New Fron-

tier," *Personnel and Guidance Journal,* Vol. 55, No. 9 (May, 1977), pp. 520–522.

14. Ludwig von Bertalanffy, *General System Theory: Foundations, Development, Applications* (George Braziller, 1969); and U. Bronfenbrenner, "Toward a Theoretical Model for the Analysis of Parent-Child Relationships in a Social Context," in *Parental Attitudes and Child Behavior,* ed. J. D. Clidewell (Charles C. Thomas, 1960).

15. Gerald Caplan, *Support Systems and Community Mental Health* (Human Science Press, 1974); Gerald Caplan, "The Family as a Support System," in *Support Systems and Mutual Help,* ed. Gerald Caplan and Marie Killilea (Grune & Stratton, 1976); R. J Burke and T. Weir, "Marital Helping Relationships: The Moderators Between Stress and Well-Being," *Journal of Psychology,* Vol. 95 (Jan., 1977), pp. 121–130; and J. Cassel, "The Contribution of the Social Environment Resistance," *American Journal of Epidemiology,* Vol. 102 (1976), pp. 107–123.

16. W. Doherty and Hamilton I. McCubbin, eds., *Family and Health* (St. Paul: National Council on Family Relations, 1984).

17. Beatrice Paolucci, O. Hall, and N. Axinn, *Family Decision Making: An Ecosystem Approach* (John Wiley & Sons, 1977); and H. A. Otto, "Criteria for Assessing Family Strength," *Family Process,* Vol. 2, No. 2 (Sept., 1963), pp. 329–337.

18. *Native Hawaiian Education Assessment Project.*

19. McCubbin, Patterson, and Lavee, *One Thousand Army Families.*

20. H. McCubbin and others, "Family Stress and Coping: A Decade Review," *Journal of Marriage and the Family,* Vol. 42, No. 4 (Nov., 1980), pp. 855–871; J. R. French, W. Rodgers, and S. Cobb, "Adjustment as a Person-Environment Fit," in *Coping and Adaptation,* ed. B. V. Coelho, D. Hamburg, and J. Adams (Basic Books, 1974); and McCubbin and Patterson (1983), "Family Transitions."

21. McCubbin, Olson, and Zimmerman, "Family Action Research."

22. Lois Pratt, *Family Structure and Effective Health Behavior The Energized Family* (Houghton Mifflin Co., 1976); Nick Stinnett and others, *Family Strengths: Positive Models for Family Life* (University of Nebraska Press, 1980); Nick Stinnett and K. Sauer, "Relationship Characteristics of Strong Families," *Family Perspective* Vol. 11, No. 4 (Fall, 1977), pp. 3–11; and D. Unger and D. Powell

"Supporting Families Under Stress: The Role of Social Networks," *Family Relations,* Vol. 29, No. 4 (Oct., 1980), pp. 566–574.

23. S. Cobb, "Social Support as a Moderator of Life Stress," *Psychosomatic Medicine,* Vol. 38, No. 5 (Sept.–Oct., 1976), pp. 300–314; and M. Pilisuk and S. Parks, "Social Support and Family Stress," in *Social Stress and the Family,* ed. McCubbin, Sussman, and Patterson.

4. THE SOCIAL MISSION OF THE FAMILY
McGINNIS AND McGINNIS

1. Dolores Curran, *Traits of a Healthy Family* (Winston Press, 1983).

2. *Declaration on Christian Education,* No. 3, in *The Documents of Vatican II* (Guild Press, 1966), p. 641.

3. Pope Paul VI, *Octogesima Adveniens,* No. 9, in *Renewing the Earth: Catholic Documents on Peace, Justice and Liberation* (Doubleday & Co., Image Books, 1977), p. 357.

4. *This Land Is Home to Me,* Part I, in *Renewing the Earth,* pp. 493–494.

5. *Northern Development: At What Cost?,* Nos. 32, 34 (Canadian Catholic Conference, 1975).

6. *Octogesima Adveniens,* No. 26, in *Renewing the Earth,* p. 366.

7. Pope Paul VI, *Populorum Progressio,* Nos. 22–23, in *Renewing the Earth,* p. 521 (United States Catholic Conference).

8. *Christian Faith and Economic Justice* (Office of the General Assembly, Presbyterian Church (U.S.A.); approved as a Study Document by the 196th General Assembly [1984]), p. 7.

9. U.S. Catholic Bishops, *The Economy: Human Dimensions,* No. 12, in *Renewing the Earth,* p. 521.

10. U.S. Catholic Bishops, *Brothers and Sisters to Us* (United States Catholic Conference, 1979), pp. 1–2.

11. Ibid., p. 6.

12. Statement of the World Council of Churches Conference on Disarmament, at Glion, Switzerland, April 9–15, 1978, quoted in *Peacemaking: The Believers' Calling* (United Presbyterian Church U.S.A.), p. 13.

13. *The Holy See on Disarmament* (1976), in *To Proclaim Peace: Religious Statements on the Arms Race,* ed. John Donaghy (Fellowship of Reconciliation, 1981), p. 27.

14. Synod of Roman Catholic Bishops, *Justice in the World,* Introduction, in *Renewing the Earth,* p. 391.

15. *Peacemaking: The Believers' Calling* (Office of the General Assembly, United Presbyterian Church U.S.A., 1980), p. 2.

16. *Educational Ministry of the Presbyterian Church (U.S.A.),* A Paper for Reflection and Discussion (Church Education Services, Program Agency, Presbyterian Church (U.S.A.), 1984), p. 19.

17. *Lineamenta: The Role of the Christian Family in the Modern World* (Washington, D.C.: U.S. Catholic Conference, 1979), p. 44.

18. *Octogesima Adveniens,* No. 48, in *Renewing the Earth,* p. 380.

19. Arlo D. Duba, "Theological Dimensions of the Lord's Supper," quoted in *Educational Ministry of the Presbyterian Church (U.S.A.),* p. 18, from *Worship in the Community of Faith,* ed. Harold M. Daniels (Joint Office of Worship, Presbyterian Church U.S.A.), (1982), pp. 108–110.

20. *Gaudium et Spes,* No. 75, in *The Documents of Vatican II,* p. 286.

21. *Peacemaking: The Believers' Calling,* pp. 4–5.

5. THE IMPORTANCE OF THE FAMILY / LEE

1. See *The Church's Educational Ministry to Families* (Board of Christian Education, United Presbyterian Church U.S.A., 1968), p. 3.

2. Cf. Brigitte Berger and Peter L. Berger, *The War Over the Family: Capturing the Middle Ground* (Doubleday & Co., Anchor Press, 1984), esp. pp. 149–167.

3. Cf. Robert N. Bellah and others, *Habits of the Heart: Individualism and Commitment in American Life* (University of California Press, 1985), pp. 85–112.

4. I am borrowing this definition from Herbert Anderson, *The Family and Pastoral Care* (Fortress Press, 1984), p. 73.

5. Helmut Thielicke, *Theological Ethics, Vol. 3: Sex* (Wm. B. Eerdmans Publishing Co., 1979), p. 142.

6. "The Church's Educational Ministry to Families" (United Presbyterian Church U.S.A., 1968), p. 7.

7. For Edwards' basic theological perspective, the following are especially pertinent: Jonathan Edwards, "Dissertation Concerning the End for Which God Created the World," in *The Works of President Edwards* (New York: Robert Carter and Brothers, 1868), Vol. 2, pp. 191ff.; "A History of the Work of Redemption," in *The Works*

of President Edwards (New York: Robert Carter and Brothers, 1868), Vol. 1, pp. 292ff.

8. See especially Edwards, "Dissertation Concerning the End for Which God Created the World."

9. See Jonathan Edwards, *Images or Shadows of Divine Things,* ed. Perry Miller (Yale University Press, 1948).

10. Edwards, "A History of the Work of Redemption," p. 306.

11. Cf. David Willis, *Daring Prayer* (John Knox Press, 1977), pp. 50ff.

12. John H. Elliott, *A Home for the Homeless: A Sociological Exegesis of 1 Peter, Its Solution and Strategy* (Fortress Press, 1981).

13. Anderson, *The Family and Pastoral Care,* pp. 17f.

14. Willis, *Daring Prayer,* p. 57.

15. For an exciting recent treatment of biblical eschatology, see J. Christiaan Beker, *Paul's Apocalyptic Gospel: The Coming Triumph of God* (Fortress Press, 1982).

16. Daniel Day Williams, *The Spirit and the Forms of Love* (Harper & Row, 1968), p. 116.

17. H. Richard Niebuhr, *The Meaning of Revelation* (Macmillan Co., 1941), p. 116.

18. Paul Tillich, *Systematic Theology* (University of Chicago Press, 1951), Vol. 1, pp. 174ff.

19. For a further discussion of the Asian immigrant context, see my "Called to Be Pilgrims: Toward a Theology Within a Korean Immigrant Context," in *The Korean Immigrant in America, Inc., 1980,* ed. B. S. Kim and S. H. Lee, pp. 37ff.

20. Quoted in Clyde A. Holbrook, *The Ethics of Jonathan Edwards* (University of Michigan Press, 1973), p. 83.

6. FAMILY PROMISES / DYKSTRA

1. See Edward Farley, *Ecclesial Man* (Fortress Press, 1975), pp. 95–98, for the discussion of the meaning and nature of marriage on which I am drawing here. Farley himself puts emphasis on the sexual intentions of marriage, defining it as "a sexually oriented commitment between male and female in which there is a mutual acceptance of responsibility for the *possible* offspring of that sexuality" (p. 96). Farley is careful to point out that "this matrix of future children is not intended as a mere biological one but as a social, economic unit characterized by qualities of affection, commitment, and endurance" (p. 97). He lifts up sexuality *and* its possible fruits

because that is what distinguishes marriage from other forms of enduring commitment. Sexuality distinguishes marriage from non-sexual forms of enduring commitment. But mere committed sexuality is not definitive enough, because there are other forms of committed sexuality which do not yet constitute marriage. "Left out" from these other forms, he says, "is the way in which futurity, the future both anticipate together, is present in the sexual commitment. The commitment to the other as a permanent mate says in effect, 'I wish to share a sexual present and sexual future with you whatever the outcome of that sexuality.' Again, this is not the positive inclination to 'have children,' but it is an implicit commitment to whatever children may appear in that future as outcomes of the sexual present. This is why the family unit is intentionally present in the constitution of the other as mate" (pp. 97–98, note 12).

One other point. If Farley is right about this understanding of what constitutes marriage, some light may be shed on why our society as a whole and the church in particular is cautious about the idea of homosexual marriage. Homosexual relationships may well be a form of committed sexuality. But because there is no potential, even, of children, there can be no promises made toward any possible future children. Hence the resistance to calling even the most enduring and committed such relationships "marriages." This may also illuminate why in biblical times, and even today, "barrenness" appears to be such a threat, both culturally and psychologically. It threatens not just the individuals involved but the institution of marriage as such, because the particular set of promises that constitute marriage become impossible to fulfill. Acceptance of childless and homosexual marriages as normative may be something we are moving more toward in our culture, and that may in many respects be good. But we should be aware that it would entail a radical change not just of practice but of the very understanding of marriage and the nature of the promises implicit in it that still prevail.

2. By defining family in terms of promise-making and by arguing that promise-making is constitutive of all families and family relationships, we do not limit family to the traditional family structures of married parents with children. By starting our analysis with the promises involved in marriage, we are making the marriage promises a primary example of, but not necessarily a prerequisite for, family. There are families that have not begun

with marriage. This does not mean that they are not families, since promise-making (very similar to the promise-making involved in marriage, I shall be arguing) also occurs there. Also, single people who do not have children are not without families. They are sons or daughters and, perhaps, brothers or sisters, and thus in family. They are just not parents.

3. Ronald M. Green, "Abortion and Promise-Keeping," *Christianity and Crisis,* Vol. 27 (1967), p. 110. I have deliberately deleted the parenthetical phrase "(the woman)" from one sentence and changed "woman" to "person" and "her" to "his or her," because where Green focuses on the woman as the initiator of the act and therefore the responsible person, I would argue that both the male and the female are (in uncoerced sexual intercourse) actors and therefore responsible.

4. The whole set of issues concerning whether or not family is constituted promissorily in cases of rape (coerced sexual intercourse), or when voluntary intercourse involves no intentions toward childbearing but either there is ignorance about sexual functioning or contraception is being used precisely in order to avoid making such promises, is all very complicated and cannot be taken up in any depth here. I might briefly indicate what I think the key issues might be in each case, however. In the case of rape, a person is in the position of having to decide whether to make promises now in the context of a situation which she did not enter promissorily in any way. In the case of ignorance about sexual functioning, a person is in the position of having to decide whether to take up responsibility for the promissory nature of his or her action that he or she had no idea at the time had any promissory dimensions. In the case of the use of contraception, it seems to me, the promissory nature of the act was known and must be faced, since it is the case that contraception does not *guarantee* that there can be no future child in relation to whom the implicit promise is expected to be fulfilled.

There are, of course, also many cases where intercourse either does not or cannot lead to childbearing. In my view, in any situation where childbearing is at all a possible result of intercourse, promise-making toward any possible offspring is implicit in the act. But the promise becomes mute when that potential is not realized (i.e., when there is no conception, for example), because there is no potential offspring to be the recipient of the implicit promise. And when there is no possibility of childbearing (when, for example, either partner is sterile), the notion of implicit promise-making toward a potential offspring is simply irrelevant. This obviously qualifies to some degree the bald statement that "sexual intercourse is in and of itself implicitly promissory."

5. Interestingly, *the Heidelberg Catechism,* in *The Constitution of the United Presbyterian Church in the United States of America,* Part I: Book of Confession, 2d edition (Philadelphia: Office of the General Assembly, United Presbyterian Church U.S.A., 1970), 4.104, confirms the idea of the promise-making of children, at least in relation to their parents, when it says:

Q. 104. What does God require in the fifth commandment?

A. That I show honor, love, and faithfulness to my father and mother and to all who are set in authority over me; that I submit myself with respectful obedience to all their careful instruction and discipline; and that I also bear patiently their failures, since it is God's will to govern us by their hand.

It does so by using the structure of commandment and obedience. My point, that promise-making is universally (i.e., not just for those who hear this commandment as part of their religious faith) constitutive in just being in family as someone's son or daughter, is thus a slightly different point. Nonetheless, the approaches are still consistent. The promissory nature constitutive of this family relationship is *presumed* by the commandment. It is not the commanding itself (or obedience or lack of obedience of it) that initiates the promissory nature of the relationship. What the presence and content of the commandment do is *(a)* make the promise-making nature of this relationship explicit and *(b)* suggest what is required for the fulfillment of it. The relation of promise-*making* to promise-*keeping,* and the function of faith in rendering promise-making explicit and in giving it content, are explored below. I wish to thank Sang Lee and Lindell Sawyers for bringing this part of the Catechism to my attention.

6. Richard K. Fenn, *Liturgies and Trials: The Secularization of Religious Language* (Pilgrim Press, 1982), p. xiii.

7. The understanding of the relationship between secularization and the undercutting of promise-making that we are exploring here is complemented by the work of Robert N. Bellah and his associates on the progressive loss of a biblical and republican "moral ecology" and the rise of "the therapeutic attitude" in American life. (See Robert N. Bellah and others, *Habits of the Heart: Individualism and Commitment in American Life* [Univer-

sity of California Press, 1985], esp. chs. 3 to 5.) The "therapeutic attitude," they say, "begins with the self, rather than with a set of external obligations. The individual must find and assert his or her true self because this self is the only source of genuine relationships to other people. External obligations, whether they come from religion, parents, or social conventions, can only interfere with the capacity for love and relatedness" (p. 98). The ultimate outcome, according to the authors, is that "in its pure form, the therapeutic attitude denies all forms of obligation and commitment in relationships, replacing them only with the ideal of full, open, honest communication among self-actualized individuals" (p. 101). Inherent in it "is a view of interpersonal relationships centered on contractual exchange, enacted in communication and negotiation, and grounded in each person's ultimate responsibility to himself or herself alone" (pp. 128–29). "By its own logic, a purely contractual ethic leaves every commitment unstable. Parties to a contract remain free to choose, and thus free to remake or break every commitment, if only they are willing to pay the price for doing so" (p. 130). All that is left to do when relationships "break down," then, is to count the costs and search for the most "cost effective" way to go on. That is what "readjustment" is.

8. *The Book of Common Worship* (Board of Christian Education of the Presbyterian Church U.S.A., 1946), pp. 183–188. Subsequent quotations from the order are taken from these pages.

9. *The Worshipbook* (Westminster Press, 1970), pp. 65–68. A committee working on a new marriage liturgy is now developing a service which, I understand, will restore these dimensions more fully.

10. *The Worshipbook*, p. 43. See *The Book of Common Worship*, p. 121, for the promises of God announced in the baptism of an infant, and pp. 126–27 for those announced in the baptism of adults. In these liturgies, the promises are not so clearly highlighted as they are in *The Worshipbook,* and the way in which they are conditional on our own promise-making and promise-keeping is more heavily stressed.

11. *The Worshipbook,* pp. 43–45, for the promises in this paragraph. The parental promise at the baptism of infants in *The Book of Common Worship* is: "Do you promise, in dependence on the grace of God, to bring up your Child in the nurture and admonition of the Lord?" (p. 122). A charge is given to the congregation, but no promise that the congregation explicitly makes is asked for (p. 123).

In the case of adult baptism, the candidate is asked: "Do you promise to make diligent use of the means of grace, to continue in the peace and fellowship of the people of God, and with the aid of the Holy Spirit to be Christ's faithful disciple to your life's end?" (p. 128). No corresponding promises are made by the congregation and no charge is given to them. *The Book of Common Worship* also has an order for "Confirmation and Admission to the Lord's Supper." In this, the confirmed answers to three questions of a promissory nature: (1) "Do you promise with the aid of the Holy Spirit to be Christ's faithful disciple to your life's end?" (2) "Do you confirm the vows taken for you in Baptism?" and (3) "Do you promise to make diligent use of the means of grace, to share faithfully in the worship and service of the Church, to give of your substance as the Lord may prosper you, and to give your whole heart to the service of Christ and His kingdom throughout the world?" (p. 132). *The Worshipbook* has an order for the confirmation and commissioning of baptized members. The promissory questions there are these: (1) "Do you intend to be his disciple, to obey his word and to show his love?" and (2) "Will you be a faithful member of this congregation, giving of yourself in every way, and will you seek the fellowship of the church wherever you may be?" (p. 49). These questions are, of course, the same as those made in the order for the baptism and commissioning of an adult.

There are no essential differences among these rubrics. The focus in both is on the vocational nature of the Christian life as discipleship and the church as the context for carrying out that vocation. *The Worshipbook* is an essential improvement on *The Book of Common Worship* here, however, because it makes more clear how the individual's promises are preceded by the promises of God and responded to by the promises of the church.

12. Such mutual pastoral care can take place in a variety of ways. Pastoral counseling by the pastor, including both individual and family counseling, would be an example, of course. But so, too, do programs such as family enrichment, marriage enrichment, and marriage encounter, and courses on marriage and family, provide both opportunities and means for such care. And I would also want to include those situations where, in mutual friendship, ordinary Christians (as part of the priesthood of all believers) provide support, counsel, care, and even instruction and discipline to each other in their family promise-making and promise-keeping. For all of us, pastors and fellow members alike, such situations raise diffi-

cult questions concerning timing and approach. When is such involvement helpful, and how? When is it simply arrogant? Difficult matters of discernment and judgment are involved here. But they call for an increased sense of responsibility rather than for avoidance.

13. In 1968, the Board of Christian Education of the United Presbyterian Church stated a position that had this kind of dualism between church and family as its unacknowledged assumption. They said that "the principal responsibility for systematic Christian education lies with the church. The church also recognizes that much fundamental learning takes place in the home and in family relationships." (See *The Church's Educational Ministry to Families,* p. 1.) The position paper went on to talk in terms of "the importance of the family to the church" and "the church's responsibility to families" as if the two were quite separate and distinct. A new paper (1985) which attempts to chart out the future of our educational ministry, entitled *Educational Ministry of the Presbyterian Church (U.S.A.): A Paper for Reflection and Discussion,* speaks of the congregation as potentially "an extended *family,* nurturing every member in Christian faith and providing the quality of support we associate with the household of faith," but then goes on to ask about ways in which the church may "more creatively and realistically support households in nurturing their members," suggesting "basic courses on living faithfully and serving justice in areas of parenting, getting adequate health care, coping with economic difficulties, living in a violent society, and exploring sexual ethics. Consistent and firm encouragement from the church facilitates family participation in cultural, recreational, service, and advocacy programs in community life" (p. 16). What at first looked like an understanding of church as an extended family involving people who are recognized at the same time to be involved in special relationships of promise-making to their kin turns out to involve the same bifurcation. The church gives courses to families and family members, teaching *them* (almost as people "other than" the church) to do what the *church* (almost as people "other than" people in families) is to do.

14. See Letty M. Russell, *Growth in Partnership* (Westminster Press, 1981).

15. Letty M. Russell, *The Future of Partnership* (Westminster Press, 1979), p. 164.

16. Ibid., pp. 54–55.

17. See 1 Corinthians 7 for Paul's advice on how early Christians ought to handle marriage relationships. He goes through a number of situations, but his guiding principle in all is articulated in v. 17: "Only, let every one lead the life which the Lord has assigned to him, and in which God has called him." On marriage between believers and nonbelievers, in particular, he makes these comments: "If any brother has a wife who is an unbeliever, and she consents to live with him, he should not divorce her. If any woman has a husband who is an unbeliever, and he consents to live with her, she should not divorce him. For the unbelieving husband is consecrated through his wife, and the unbelieving wife is consecrated through her husband. Otherwise, your children would be unclean, but as it is they are holy. But if the unbelieving partner desires to separate, let it be so; in such a case the brother or sister is not bound. For God called us to peace. Wife, how do you know whether you will save your husband? Husband, how do you know whether you will save your wife?" (vs. 12–16).

What Paul seems to have in mind here might be put, in our terms, this way: If the promises of the marriage can live simultaneously with the promises of the faith, then the marriage can and should be sustained. From the point of view of the believer's faith promises, there is nothing to prevent this. But the believer's faith promises may, from the point of view of the unbeliever, so undercut the marriage promises that the marriage cannot be sustained. It is interesting that it is the *un*believer who is called upon to decide.

18. *The Church's Educational Ministry to Families* (Board of Christian Education, United Presbyterian Church U.S.A., 1968), p. 1.

7. FAMILY MINISTRIES AND
THE LOCAL CHURCH / IKELER

1. Letty Cottin Pogrebin, *Family Politics: Love and Power on an Intimate Frontier* (McGraw-Hill Book Co., 1983).

2. See the section "The Bible" in The Confession of 1967, *The Constitution of the Presbyterian Church (U.S.A.),* Part I: The Book of Confessions (Office of the General Assembly, 1983), and the section "The Bible Is the Written Word of God" in A Declaration of Faith, *The Proposed Book of Confessions* (Presbyterian Church U.S., 1976).

3. From the section "The Relationship Between Man and Woman," The Confession of 1967. Inclusive language text prepared by Cynthia A. Jarvis and Freda A. Gardner.

4. James B. Nelson, *Embodiment: An Approach to Sexuality and Christian Theology* (Pilgrim Press, 1978).

5. For discussions of "family systems," see J. C. Wynn, *Family Therapy in Pastoral Ministry* (Harper & Row, 1982), and Maslow and Duggan, *Family Connections: Parenting Your Grown Children* (Doubleday & Co., 1982).

6. Hamilton I. McCubbin and Marilyn A. McCubbin, chapter 3 in this book.

7. See the McGinnises' chapter 4 in this book, especially the last two sections.

8. Both Guides are available for a nominal fee from Presbyterian Publishing House, Presbyterian Center, 341 Ponce de Leon Avenue, NE, Atlanta, Georgia 30365.

9. Joe Leonard, Jr., *Planning Family Ministry: A Guide for a Teaching Church* (Judson Press, 1982).

10. From the section "The Bible," The Confession of 1967. Inclusive language text prepared by Cynthia A. Jarvis and Freda A. Gardner.

11. From the section "The Bible Is the Written Word of God," in A Declaration of Faith, *The Proposed Book of Confessions* (The General Assembly of the Presbyterian Church in the U.S., 1977).

12. Francis E. Ringer, "Comments on the Present Attention to the Family," in *The Family Album* (Resources for Family Life Ministries) United Church Board for Homeland Ministries, 1986), pp. 1–3, 7, 8–9, 11–12. (For added insight into the new liberation hermeneutic, see Robert McAfee Brown, *Unexpected News: Reading the Bible with Third World Eyes,* 1984, and *Theology in a New Key: Responding to Liberation Themes,* 1978, both Westminster Press.)

13. See also Rosemary Ruether, "An Unrealized Revolution: Searching Scripture for a Model of the Family," in *Christianity and Crisis,* Dec. 31, 1983, pp. 399–404.

14. Judith Kovacs, in chapter 1 in this book.

15. See catalog listing of Franciscan films. Other current reliable sexuality resources include the following: The substantial sex education series published in 1982 by Concordia Lutheran Press, Minneapolis, Minn.; the Youth Elect Series in *Christian Education:*

Shared Approaches, for younger and older teens and their parents; and the seven-session adult study *Growing in Marriage,* available from Presbyterian Church (U.S.A.), P.O. Box 868, William Penn Annex, Philadelphia, Pa. 19105.

16. Joe Vaughn and Ron Klug, *New Life for Men: A Book for Men and Women Who Care About Them* (Augsburg Publishing House, 1984).

17. Diane Tennis, *Is God the Only Reliable Father?* (Westminster Press, 1985).

18. James E. Dittes, *The Male Predicament: On Being a Man Today* (Harper & Row, 1985).

Ghost Ranch Symposium on "Faith and Families"

FOCUSING STATEMENT

Lindell Sawyers

"Family" is a synonym for nurturing and mutually supportive relationships that endure over time. Family refers to the persons you feel bound to and on whom you rely.

In a more basic sense, family is that group of persons with whom we are linked as parents or children or siblings or kin, by birth or by adoption. Each of us has a family in this sense —for better or for worse. Some families are bound together in love. Others do not get along with each other at all and disperse, rarely to meet again. Families bless and families hurt. For our entire lives we live out the implications of the gifts and deprivations of family—feeding on the reservoir of love once tendered, and transcending the lacks and hurts of love lost or withheld.

Each of us in some sense is family for someone else—our own parents or children, or those near us who need to be cared for and touched. Each of us is potentially family to a neighbor, a workmate, an elderly person in a nursing home, a battered woman in need of shelter, a man or a woman without a job. And there are families of choice, persons not

Reprinted, with adaptations, from *Concern*, Vol. 27, No. 1 (January 1985). Used with permission of the publisher, United Presbyterian Women, Presbyterian Church (U.S.A.).

"related" who live together to fulfill social, economic, and personal needs.

Today in American culture families are changing. Traditional family patterns and patriarchal systems are giving way to more egalitarian styles of family living. Relationships rather than roles define who we are in families.

The ties that bind us together in neighborhood and workplace—even in church fellowship—have seriously weakened. Persons die in unheated rooms, are assaulted while busy commuters hurry by, live out their lives in the isolation of institutions—without nurturing, supportive relationships that endure. Most distressing of all, many in families, who should be bound together by love, are trapped in abuse or violence—adults abusing children, husbands abusing wives, sometimes wives their husbands.

Recent census figures reveal drastic changes in American households. The observations below arise out of these figures, but the numbers on a page conceal rather than reveal the dramas and challenges that such changes present:

- Over half the women with preschool children are participating in the labor market whether or not they are married.
- The number of smaller families is increasing because couples are having fewer children.
- Marriage is being delayed and there is indication that men and women are being more deliberate about their choice of mate.
- It is more common for couples to live together in a temporary or even long-term arrangement before marriage.
- It is more common for individuals to choose not to marry.
- Divorce has become an acceptable way of terminating a marriage relationship, and the reasons for divorce increasingly are related to questions of personal satisfaction and fulfillment.
- While a significant number of divorced persons will remarry, perhaps even a larger percentage of them will redivorce.

- A significant number of divorced persons will decide to remain single or to live together without marriage.
- There is an increase in the rise of female-headed families, with one income, leading often to stress and deprivation for children.
- The one-parent family, it appears, is becoming a major form for raising children in the United States.
- More married couples are exercising the option to remain childless. The fertility rate is falling dramatically. The number of live births per thousand women between ages fifteen and forty-four was 118 in 1960 and 68 in 1982.
- Alternate life-styles are widely accepted by the general population and are reinforced by the mass media.

For the more privileged in our society, it has been a time of new freedom and heightened expectations; the trends reflect the way we have chosen to live. There are also ominous economic clouds on the horizon. Our high expectations may be on a collision course with a period of shrinking possibilities. Meanwhile, large numbers of black and Hispanic citizens have been barred from the economic well-being enjoyed by other Americans, and their family life has borne the brunt of inadequate income and its attendant distresses. Their courage and adaptability in the face of such odds is instructive for all families.

The changing patterns of marriage and family are having a profound impact on children. Obviously, separation and divorce present a crisis for all family members, and children are especially vulnerable as they experience the drawing apart of those they love and depend on. Congregations have a special opportunity to be supportive and to provide counseling to adults and children at the time of divorce and during the critical months that follow.

Experts on family life and child-rearing are not of one mind regarding the long-term results of one-parent family styles, and the two-income family. Recent periodical literature has pointed to studies indicating that mothers who work provide a positive role model for children at home.

They see their mothers as competent in the outside world as well as in the home ("The Working Mother as Role Model," *New York Times Magazine,* September 9, 1984). Other commentators suggest that very young children and their parents are often both losers in family settings where either the single parent or both parents work. Important events and milestones in the child's early years may be missed (first steps, first words), and the child, while well cared for in a day care setting, may nevertheless not receive the amount of attention and loving contact that a home environment might provide. It will take time to sort these factors out. The freedom and fulfillment that new family styles provide may produce happier parents with fewer frustrations to vent on children. The stress of coping with home, parenthood, and career, on the other hand, may overflow onto children and lead to severe emotional and behavioral problems ("Single Parents Who Raise Children Feel Stretched Thin by Home, Job," *Wall Street Journal,* September 28, 1984).

A warm and caring church community is in a unique position to minister to various kinds of families and to meet certain needs that are not fulfilled in the home setting. Within the family of faith there are surrogate aunts and uncles, parents and grandparents, male and female role models. Church-based day care programs can exhibit a qualitative difference as Christian love and care are expressed in programs for the very young.

In a time of rapid change with its distress, dislocation, and opportunity, Christians are called to an intentional ministry to and with families—all kinds of families. We are also called to affirm our membership in "the household of faith," by which our lives are nurtured and sustained. We are called as well to affirm our membership in the universal family of God —the human family—and to speak and act in the name of justice on behalf of all persons in their struggle to be whole.

Contributors

JUDITH KOVACS is Visiting Assistant Professor of Religious Studies, University of Virginia, Charlottesville, Virginia

JANET HUBER LOWRY is Assistant Professor of Sociology, Austin College, Sherman, Texas

HAMILTON I. McCUBBIN is Dean of the School of Family Resources and Consumer Sciences, University of Wisconsin, Madison, Wisconsin. MARILYN A. McCUBBIN is Assistant Professor, Gustavus Adolphus College, St. Peter, Minnesota.

JAMES and KATHLEEN McGINNIS are founders and co-coordinators of the National Parenting for Peace and Justice Network, with offices in St. Louis, Missouri

SANG H. LEE is Assistant Professor of Theology, and Director, Program for Asian-American Theology and Ministry, Princeton Theological Seminary, Princeton, New Jersey

CRAIG DYKSTRA is Thomas W. Synnott Professor of Christian Education, Princeton Theological Seminary, Princeton, New Jersey

CAROL ROSE IKELER is Director of the Office of Family Ministries, General Assembly Mission Board, Presbyterian Church (U.S.A.), Atlanta, Georgia